# FINALLY FIND FREEDOM

## HOW TO BREAK THE 12 CHAINS HOLDING YOU BACK AND FIND MORE FREEDOM IN LIFE AND BUSINESS

---

**PHILIP WRIDE**

ISBN: 978-1-7392135-2-7

# Contents

# INTRODUCTION

As I slowly opened my eyes, I could hear the murmurs from the crowd. It wasn't a big crowd but there were some cheers and the general chatter you get on the touchline. I was lying on my back and looking up into the sky. It was a beautiful blue sky on a hot and sunny Friday afternoon in Dubai.

It was January 2020 and I was playing rugby at the Dubai Sevens Rugby Stadium for a local team in the local league. We were losing badly and it had been pretty much the last play of the game. I was still committed to doing my job.

Rolling on to my side to prepare to stand up, I could see my opponent also laid out on the grass a few feet away. He was still coming round from the collision between us.

Moments earlier, I had been preparing myself for the impact. My opponent was running full speed in my direction and my responsibility was to stop him from scoring. The position I was playing was "full back". If you are unfamiliar with rugby, it's a position that's a bit like the last line of defence. If an opponent breaks through or kicks over your line of players, it's your job to sweep around and try to nullify the threat or start a counter-attack.

I was lining this guy up to tackle him and stop him from scoring. I edged across the field and judged his running line so I could meet him head-on. Knees slightly bent, I was rocking on the balls of my feet so I could drive forward into the collision as he kept coming closer.

*Whack!*

We collided.

From the position I'd set myself in, I worked to wrap my arms around his legs in the traditional tackle style and take him to the ground.

The problem was that at the speed he was running and the movement I made, I got my head in the wrong position. Normally your head is meant to be nicely cushioned against the softest part of the opponent — their bum.

This time I didn't quite get to that position and my head was struck full-on by his thigh as he was pumping his legs to try and run through me. We both hit the ground.

As I continued my attempt to stand up, I stumbled a little to the left and then made for the edge of the pitch while the game was still going on around me.

I can't remember who it was but someone asked me if I was okay and, full of bravado, I said that my neck was a little stiff. The next thing I knew the whistle had gone for full time and all the players were walking off the pitch and into the crowd and changing rooms.

I slowly walked to the changing room, teetering from side to side, had a slow shower and tried to dress myself. It wasn't a sharp pain in my neck and shoulders, more of a dull ache, like the type you get a few days after a really hard gym session. The type you think will subside in a few days because you've pulled all your muscles and they just need a bit of time to recover and repair. But I'm not going to lie, it was hard to turn my head at all, as if all the muscles together had decided to go on holiday and my head was just fixed in position looking forward.

After changing, I got in the car to drive home. Let me tell you, this was one of the most difficult drives because I couldn't turn my head. Looking in my side mirrors was a challenge — I had to keep flicking my eyes from left to right rather than move my head. And yes, I know what you are thinking, I was an idiot to get in the car and do the 40-minute drive home and I agree, but at the time I didn't realise how tough it would be.

The drive back was slow. I took it steadily and precisely because I couldn't turn my head.

Sleep was tough.

I couldn't roll onto my side because that involved moving my head.

The next day, I visited a pharmacy and bought myself a neck brace to support my neck while my muscles recovered. I wore this for days and even wore it for sleeping.

The club that I was playing for had a physio we could visit, so in a bid to loosen off the muscles and stimulate tissue repair, I visited the physio. They attempted to move my head and neck, manipulate it, loosen off the muscles, and work on the nerves a little bit. There is a nerve cluster in the back of your head just at the top of your neck.

I repeated this process for 7 weeks, but my neck and shoulders were still really stiff. It had become easier to sleep as I had found positions that worked or ways to move my body while I was wearing the neck brace.

Finally, with the physio at a loss for why my neck and shoulders were still so stiff, he suggested I go and get some scans. I found a hospital that was on the list for the insurance I had and booked an appointment.

After completing the scans, I sat down with the consultant to get the feedback. As he started talking, time seemed to stop.

C5-C6.

Broken.

Plate and screws.

Those were the words I heard.

The impact of the tackle had broken my vertebrae at the C5-C6 section which is towards the bottom of the neck. The consultant wanted to do surgery to insert a plate and screws into my neck.

I remember listening to what the surgery would involve and shutting down mentally and physically.

The procedure would need to have incisions in the front and back of my neck — they would do one side and then flip me over to do the other side, for what could be a total of anywhere from 3 to 6 hours depending on how things went.

I'm a stubborn guy and knew I didn't want to have the surgery. There was a risk of it going wrong, although the consultant said it was still a better option than leaving it and doing nothing. But there was something else that contributed to the decision — my situation and the world situation — I didn't have the money to pay for it myself. The world was also shutting down because COVID had started. This was in March 2020.

So I decided against the surgery.

When I broke my ankle playing rugby at university just before my 21$^{st}$ birthday, the surgery that was suggested was optional. I opted against it and my ankle healed. Don't get me wrong, it's not perfect and I still get pain in it every now and again.

But this experience with my ankle led me to believe that my body was strong enough to heal my neck.

I was putting my faith and belief in myself.

I kept wearing the neck brace for a period after that visit to the consultant and over time, the pain in my neck and shoulders reduced to a point where I stopped wearing it. The muscles had loosened off and I could turn my head again. Sleeping was more comfortable overall, and I felt like everything was getting back to normal.

And when I say getting back to normal, I mean apart from the odd lightning bolt of pain through my right shoulder area and across the right side of my chest into the middle of my chest. I didn't know what was causing this, and it was at random moments, so I just put up with it and carried on with life.

Eighteen months later, I went to visit a different consultant and to get a fresh set of scans.

I'd already seen a respected sports physio in the hospital, who had worked with international rugby players, and he referred me to this specialist spinal consultant.

When I sat down with the consultant to review the scans, he had a look of amazement on his face. He explained that he'd never seen anything like it.

After the referral from the specialist sports physio, the consultant had done some research on similar cases but everything he found was about people waiting a maximum of 3 weeks and then having the surgery they needed. He hadn't found any examples of people being silly enough to not have surgery.

The scans revealed that my body had created new bone around the break in my neck. The circled area in this image shows the new bone that had grown on my vertebrae.

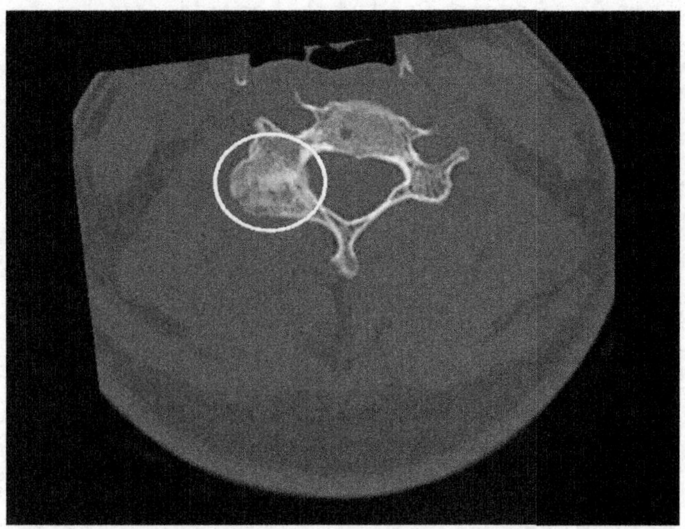

*This is the scan of the vertebrae I broke and how my body had grown new bone around the break*

He manipulated my neck a bit and got me to twist my head from side to side, up and down, to check the range of movement. He told me that he was really happy with the range of movement I had, and the strength in my neck, and that my neck was virtually like that of someone without the injury. The word he actually used was *miracle*.

The way my body had healed based on the type of injury was a miracle.

There were, however, a few minor points he highlighted. The vertebrae was twisted during the impact so my head is no longer straight on, it twists to the right slightly. And this twist also impinges the nerve in my neck. Which explained why I was randomly getting sharp shooting pains through my right shoulder and chest like a lightning bolt had struck me.

But these were things I could live with. I was used to having niggles from other injuries.

On the whole, the belief I had in the power to heal had been rewarded and I was able to continue with my life.

And although I've started with the full story about my neck, this is only a part of what happened and what changed for me.

I was feeling stuck, I was frustrated, and my business was struggling. It was *my* business but the nature of it was largely project-based. Sometimes, it was a live event project. Other times, it was a consultancy project to create a strategy for a brand or a government. My background is 20 years working in the video game industry so that's what I was focused on. Gaming tournaments and events, strategy for how a brand could enter the market based on their objectives—that sort of thing.

I'd also set the business up in a way where I built project teams. This kept my overheads low with no fixed staffing costs but it also meant most of the time, it was just me trying to grow the business and to service any projects that came through. There were periods when I would be so focused on delivering a project that I didn't give time to business development, and so when the project finished, I suddenly had a big gap with no next project lined up.

As COVID started locking down the world in 2020—well before I got my second set of scans and found out that my neck had healed—all the event proposals I was working on suddenly disappeared because the event world stopped.

Events had been 50% of my business at that point and I would do events for clients in and around the video game industry and esports. I was able to do some online projects, but a lot of people were tightening or cutting budgets and things were tough.

I knew I needed to make changes to the business and to my life. In the early part of lockdowns in Dubai, we had to get approval slips to go out and get groceries and there was a curfew each night while they disinfected the streets. My focus switched to just getting by each day and trying to get any projects I could.

Sometime in the spring of 2021, I saw an advert on YouTube for a personal development course and thought to myself, '*What have I got to lose?*' The business was still struggling, even though the lockdowns and restrictions had started to be relaxed.

I started the course and one of the questions that it asked me to think about was impact — it was part of Tim Han's Life Mastery Achievers or LMA. What would be said about me at my funeral and what positive impact had I made on the world?

This got me thinking because up to that point, I hadn't really made any real contribution. I was supporting clients, and doing projects, but they didn't serve a larger purpose. I had spent the best part of 20 years working in an industry that interested and excited me — video games. I started playing at the age of 7 and from those early beginnings, I've been able to work for EA SPORTS on the FIFA10 and FIFA11 versions of the popular video game, been invited to No. 10 Downing Street, written 4 pages for the 2009 Gamer's Edition of the Guinness Book of World Records and completed various media interviews for magazines, TV and radio. But still, there had been no real contribution to a bigger cause.

And the universe works in mysterious ways.

While working through the exercises in the course and attempting to find my purpose and how I could positively impact the world, a random opportunity presented itself.

My partner is a teacher, and she was teaching 9-year-old girls. We were chatting over dinner one night, and she mentioned she needed the lesson plan and resources for a maths lesson the next day because there was nothing on the system from her colleagues.

I knew that all her students were into the video game called "Among Us" so I suggested creating a lesson based around the game. "Among Us" is a game where players take the role of crewmates or an imposter. The imposter goes around secretly trying to bump off the crewmates, and the crewmates work to unmask the imposter or complete enough tasks to win.

The lesson was about perimeter in maths so I suggested that she tasked her students with redesigning the level in the game and all the rooms. This way, they could think about perimeter and layouts to meet the objectives of the lesson and learning.

Thirty minutes later, we had a lesson plan and some basic resources.

The next day, I got a message from her with a few simple words — "They love this Among Us stuff."

It even had one of those emojis in the message, the one with the monkey holding its hands over its eyes.

That's when I knew my experience from the video game industry could be used to create resources for maths and to help improve the maths skills of children who had spent lockdown playing games.

I dived into creating resources and frameworks — which is where the PARROT Framework comes from. This is a framework for looking at any video game, identifying key features or mechanics, and then using those as the context for creating maths questions.

It enabled me to create maths questions based on games like Fortnite, FIFA, Among Us, Minecraft, and Roblox.

Having created this model, I started to write a book about it to help parents and teachers create their own maths resources. But, while I was having conversations with parents about the resources I had already created, there was a topic that kept coming up — managing screen time.

I realised that if I didn't help parents address the challenges with managing screen time, I wouldn't be able to support them with the maths. So, I set about uncovering tactics and strategies for managing screen time more effectively, and for managing online safety as well.

From interviews with parents, child psychologists and industry experts across the world, I created some new models and frameworks for parents to use and started sharing those. These all became the first half of the book 'Watch Us Play', with the second half of the book talking about the PARROT Framework and creating maths resources.

But this wasn't the end of the journey.

I published the book on Amazon in December 2022 and throughout 2023, I started doing more things to support parents. I hosted a 1-hour online training session in April and then in June 2023, I hosted a 4-day online challenge for parents where I walked and talked them through some of the tactics for managing screen time, why kids love to play games, how a child's brain works, and other important things I felt they should know.

I know you might be starting to question, how does all this relate to finding freedom in life and the subject of this book? Stay with me here.

As I was creating the slides for this 4 days' worth of training, I created another model and framework. You can probably see a recurring theme here. Having dived into personal development and learning new things, I spent some time learning about ways of teaching, and models/frameworks were a topic that came up regularly. Models and frameworks were a way to share information with an audience in a digestible format but also for moments such as if the teacher got side-tracked by a question, they could just go back to the step in the framework and then carry on to the next step.

The model and framework I created for this 4-day online training was about the 12 hidden things that parents aren't aware of that impact their ability to manage screen time and online safety for their kids.

But as I looked at this framework, I realised it was actually a model for life. It was the 12 chains that hold us back, and I recognised several of these chains in my own life.

Having been an entrepreneur since the age of 16, freedom has been my highest-level value, the thing that's most important to me. I've turned projects down because they would take away my view of freedom and I've also done the same with jobs and opportunities. You could argue that it is what contributed to the business struggling and you may well be right, but that's all ifs, buts, and maybes.

This '12 chain' model outlined the things that hold us back and from the previous work I'd done, I already had a 4-step model for making a change. By combining them, I now had a model that focused on the things that would help people find freedom in their own lives.

I knew this deep down because when I looked at the model, I could see the chains I had broken in my own life and the changes I had made since breaking my neck.

In the 3 and a half years since breaking my neck, and the 2 years from starting personal development, I'd overcome fear and a knowledge gap to write and publish my first book. I'd started doing more public speaking to gain more confidence. I did away with caring about perception in parts of my life — I'd never been one to shy away from wearing shirts with flower patterns or brightly coloured trousers or shorts because that was my style — I didn't care what other people thought. At one event, the host of a discussion panel commended me for being a guest on the panel while wearing a flowery shirt and pink shorts.

I'd launched a podcast and started reaching out to people to invite them to be a guest. I'd given up alcohol because I was tired of feeling rubbish for 2 days after drinking. I'd thrown myself into uncomfortable situations by doing workshops, doing more public speaking, and teaching in schools, something I'd never done before.

In one of the personal development exercises, I made a list of all the things that made me feel good and that I wanted to do — one of them was to be outside more. The majority of my work up to that point had involved me being stuck behind a computer, writing presentations, and being on calls. The decision I made was to start walking more. At the time of writing this book, I lived in an area overlooking a golf course and so I started walking to the golf course a few days a week, sitting and having a coffee and making notes for projects and my business. I also used these trips to listen to podcasts and the coffee time to write my first book.

I was combining multiple activities at the same time while also following through on something I decided I wanted to do.

These were all changes I had made or things I had done to make changes in my life.

I was already starting to live the model and framework that I had created and now I'm sharing it with you. I'm not perfect in any shape or form, but my hope is that as you read through this book, you will see opportunities to change your own life for the better and finally find the freedom you desire.

And to support you as you continue to read, I've prepared a resource pack — it has some worksheets, reference points, and additional tools/resources that will help you on your journey to freedom. You can download it for free at www.finallyfindfreedom.com/resources.

Now let's quickly talk about how this book is structured and how best to use it.

The book is split into 3 parts. Part 1 looks at the vision for your future and the importance of mindset, desires, and beliefs. This section on its own can be used as a guiding light, north star, or reference point. The activities contained within these initial chapters can immediately help you make a shift in your own life as I've distilled my experiences, the books that I've read, the events and training I've participated in, and some of the thinking I've done so that you don't have to.

The second part of the book, and in my view the key part, is about the 12 chains. There is a chapter for each chain so that we can explore them together. The reason I've done this is that you and I are different. The chain that I struggle with the most might be easy for you, and vice versa. But once you know what the 12 chains are and how they fit together, you'll be in a better position to utilise Part 3 of this book which focuses on the 4 steps you can take to break through a chain and move forward with your life.

I also want to highlight that a lot of the book uses the reference "we" because I'm talking about us as a collective and because I'm still working to break through some of the chains. As I move to a new level, sometimes the chains come back — the fear of taking a new uncomfortable action into a new space or the perceptions of me by other people as I evolve. So I've written this in the sense that we, together as a group of people, can do this because "we" all have the power to change, improve, and move forward.

And I feel I should put a little disclaimer here — some chains might be easier to break than others, some may be quick, and others may take repeated effort, but once you have the vision for your life and are committed to it, this repeated effort starts to just become a part of who you are. Like anything in life, some things are easy, others are hard. Being a doctor or lawyer takes repeated effort over multiple years. Being a star athlete is exactly the same — but for the people who have a vision for achieving any of those 3, they know they have to put in repeated effort to get to where they want to be.

And speaking of vision, let us now move to Part 1 of this book and create the TALE of your life.

# Part 1
# Creating Your Dream Life

For us to effectively follow a path, we need to know where we are going and that's why I've written this part of the book first. It's important to document and understand what we want in our lives because that will give us an initial destination to aim for.

It might not be our final destination because we change and the world changes around us but it's better than having no destination or direction in mind.

The first chapter in this part of the book will take you through the exercise of creating the TALE of your life. This exercise is to help you start to write down and document 4 areas of the life you want, which for ease we will call a future vision, and the things you are working towards.

From there, we take a whirlwind tour of topics like desire, happiness, freedom, and mindset. I believe these are important things to position early on because they will be referenced throughout the rest of the book and in combination, all of them play a role in helping us achieve the life of our dreams. On the flipside, they can also sabotage everything we try to do, so the sooner we can get a handle on them the better off we'll be.

Throughout Part 1, and the rest of the book, I also reference some of the authors and books that have personally influenced me over the past few years and I've picked out extracts to help support or highlight a point.

There are also exercises and activities for you to do throughout the book so that you can start making changes in your life and work towards the vision you have for your life.

And speaking of future vision — this is our starting point and the direction of travel.

—

**Download the free resource pack!**

The free resource pack supporting this book and the exercises you will go through in the next chapters include worksheets and other supporting material.

You can download it for free using the link below or by scanning the QR code:

https://www.finallyfindfreedom.com/resources

# What's the TALE of Your Life?

This might sound like a cheesy title and I could have written the word story — what's the story of your life — but there's a good reason I've written TALE all in capitals and it's because it's an easy model for us to use when talking about our vision, dreams, and desires.

Throughout the personal development journey that I've been on, I completed exercises like creating a vivid vision, the 3MiQ (Most Important Questions) from Mindvalley, looked at the 12 parts of Lifebook, and even created a basic vision board of some printed-out images I stuck on my desk.

And from looking at all of these, I realised I wanted something quick and easy that would give me an immediate kick in the right direction. I'll hold my hands up and say that yes, I'm one of those people who sometimes looks for instant gratification. I grew up playing video games and they are all designed in such a way that it is easy to get little hits of dopamine and gratification as you win a battle, complete a level, or solve a puzzle.

Having something quick and easy as a signpost that I could refer to just made sense for how my brain works. And if it was quick and easy, it would also be easy to update as my life and situation changed. It would also be something that was quick and easy for other people to use in their own lives and update as they make progress.

When I started writing the first draft of this book, I did some research asking people about their goals and visions for the future, how they would like to spend their time, how they rated themselves in terms of their current life situation, and how close they were to achieving their goals and reaching the vision.

There were a couple of interesting things that came out of the research. One of the biggest themes or trends was about family. Many respondents wrote that more time with family was a big driver for them, and the two biggest things holding them back from achieving their goals were time and money.

Time and money are an interesting paradox in the way the world is currently structured. We use time to get money but then have no time left to do the things we want, or we have greater amounts of free time but have less money to do the things we want, like spending time with family. The people who break free of this are those who create a new reality for themselves, who break free of the 9-5 cycle and create their own businesses, structured in a way where they get to strike that balance between time and money.

Up to the moment of writing this book, I was regularly in a situation where I had time but no money because the businesses I had created were focused on delivering projects or on consulting for a fixed period of time. When one project finished, there was often a gap because when I was involved in delivering the project, I didn't have the time to seek and secure new business, or the next project to roll into. This is the situation I was in with my first business back in 2008 and 2009 when we got into the housing crash. Because I was focused on servicing the clients that I had when they decided to tighten budgets, I was one of the people who was "nice to have" so got cut off and my situation went from having a few clients and projects to having nothing. Now I look back and see it was part of the journey but at the time, it was really tough to accept and muddle through.

If you are reading this as someone who feels stuck and frustrated in the 9-5 and wants to move away from that structure, or you are just starting as an entrepreneur with your own project or business, my advice, for whatever it is worth, is to think about how you can create something with a lot of consistency, like a service-based business, or something where you create assets that you can sell but that doesn't always require a lot of time. Otherwise, there is a risk you create something where you give yourself a job and work 70 hours a week and still have no extra time to spend with family, or on the activities you'd prefer to be doing. Or you go to the other extreme, like I did, which is severe peaks and troughs and so you spend your time chasing the next project or client.

When I created the model which this book is focused on, I took a step back and re-assessed everything. I recreated the vision for my future, what I wanted to achieve, and how I wanted to live and spend my time. I stopped doing some things in the business or made decisions to move away from certain aspects, like responding to RFPs, and instead focused on building recurring services or assets. There was an opportunity to build a course related to the video game and esports industry that I had been a part of and have someone else put a budget into marketing it. This enabled me to create an asset that could generate revenue without me always spending against it and without needing lots of time. I spent the summer of 2023 creating all the videos and supporting resources for this course which was an 8-week short course on a part of the video game industry that I'd been working in for over 20 years — events and tournaments.

You may think this is ironic given that my business was struggling because I was focused on events and had peaks and troughs of projects but all that experience and hardship meant that I was in a position to create the course (I had the time freedom after completing a project), and I knew exactly what needed to be in the course to help others.

Dean Graziosi and Tony Robbins talk about the self-education industry and how packaging your knowledge and experience into courses, workshops, masterminds and coaching options can be a way of finding that balance between time and money freedom. This is what I've done with the 12 chains model, the Chained to Champion project, and the Freedom Hunters Club, and is ultimately the purpose of this book — to share the knowledge and experience with you in a way that gives you a resource you can use to support you in life.

But why is having a vision for the future important? As human beings, we take comfort in certainty, in stability, in the things we know and recognise. On the flip side, we are also the only animal species that we know of that is developed enough to think about the future, dream, and envisage what might and can happen.

A vision or set of dreams enables us to think about what can be while also looking at the gap between where we are currently and where we want to be. There are countless stories of people rising from poverty into positions of prosperity, people overcoming disabilities and near-fatal accidents to thrive, and people changing their circumstances before going on to change the world.

All of this is possible, but only if we know what we want or where we are trying to get to. It also enables us to decide what we won't tolerate or agree to. Michael Jordan is famous for not compromising; he worked harder than anyone else to achieve his dreams. He wouldn't sink to the level of his teammates — they either came up to his level or they moved on — because he knew what was needed for him to achieve his dreams and his vision.

Edison had a vision for what he wanted to invent, and we know the story of his 10,000 attempts to create the lightbulb. His vision enabled him to stay on course because he knew where he was trying to get to and what he wanted to achieve. Henry Ford was the same; he had a vision for what he wanted to create and stayed focused on that vision until he achieved it.

If you already have a vision for your life and future, then I applaud you. You're already a step ahead, but I'm going to walk you through the TALE model so that you can see how easy it is and then decide for yourself whether to stick or twist — stick with your existing model or switch to this.

There's no right way or wrong way, and I won't be offended if you use a different model. In fact, I'll be delighted for you because it shows you're making a commitment to yourself. You're creating a vision and that's the key starting point to making changes in your life and achieving the freedom you want.

So, what exactly is the TALE model that I've been talking about?

TALE is a grid of 4 quadrants and each quadrant enables you to write down your wants and desires in 4 different areas.

**T = Time**
**A = Activities**
**L = Location**
**E = Experiences**

You might see some similarities to the 3MiQ if you've ever done that exercise but having a grid of 4 has a nice symmetry.

The Time quadrant is where you write down how you want to use your time. Do you want a 4-hour morning routine like Caren whom I interviewed on my Unchained podcast? Do you want to have lunch out with friends every Sunday afternoon? Do you want to sit by the beach in the evening and listen to the waves?

This is your opportunity to detail exactly how you would like to use your time, the same 24 hours that we all have and that the majority of us spend working for someone else.

In his book, The Code of The Extraordinary Mind, author Vishen Lakhiani, founder of Mindvalley, summed it up really well. Here's an extract:

> ***"We devote our waking hours to work, to earn a living so we can continue living a life where we spend the majority of our waking hours at work — it's a human hamster wheel."***

And if we are creating a vision for our future then we should be the ones in control of our time and how we choose to spend it. Yes, we might have some responsibilities or projects that we want to work on and that are important to us but for the rest of the time, how do you want to spend your time?

In the online communities I've been a part of, there are people who have built businesses around creating an audience on places like X (formerly Twitter) and then monetising through courses and coaching. Others provide ghost-writing services where they write content for other people and have clients who pay them a monthly service fee. Others are editing videos and writing captions for short-form content and doing that for a monthly fee for multiple clients.

The way these people have structured their businesses, and the services they offer, means they don't have to spend all the hours working in the business. Some of the work they outsource or delegate so one of their early objectives was to get to a point where the business had enough revenue to be able to do that, and so the founder bought back their time to focus on other things. This is one example of how we can think about the Time quadrant. How we set our lives up so that we have the time to spend with family, or on the things that interest us and that we want to do.

The Activities quadrant plays alongside the Time quadrant. What activities do you want to be able to do on a regular basis? This could be a social club, lunches, hobbies, projects, or anything else. The important thing is that activities in this TALE Grid are about the things you want to do regularly, not a singular type of experience which is what the Experience quadrant is focused on.

Here's a useful way to think about things for the Activities quadrant — what do you want to spend your time doing if everyone else is working, and what do you want to spend your time doing if the rest of the world suddenly has free time like at the traditional weekend?

Think about activities that energise you and make you feel good. Feelings are important. If you write down activities that don't excite you or make you smile when you think about them, then sadly there's no place for them on this grid. Harsh but true.

Someone once asked me, as we were working on their TALE Grid together, what about the activities that you don't yet know that you enjoy, want to do more of, or if you currently have no hobbies? It's a great question and my reply stunned them. I told them to write in the Time quadrant how much time per day they wanted to be able to explore new activities and find the things that excite them and that they enjoy.

Being able to do this and having the time would support them in two different areas — firstly, they would grow by trying new activities and seeing what makes them feel good. Secondly, they would be able to take the blank canvas in front of them and mould it however they wanted in terms of the time they allocated to those different activities.

In my Time quadrant, I have things like spending more time on scuba diving, writing, travelling, paddle boarding, and skiing. These are the activities that make me feel good and that I want to have as a regular part of my life. Now I recognise that some of these activities may be easier to do than others, and some are location-dependent, but the main point is that I've identified the things that make me feel good and the things that I want to spend more time doing.

Next, we move to the Location quadrant. Is there somewhere you dream of living? A type of house? What does it look like? Or do you want to be able to hop from place to place? Whichever you choose, this is where you can write down that vision. Describe the location you want to live or the list of places you want to be able to jump between.

My vision for location has always been a house on the beach so I can sit and listen to the waves, but I don't have a specific location in mind at the moment. I'll know it when I find it, but until then I still know what I'm working towards — having the ability to access or buy a house on a beach. And I haven't written a specific location down because there are many types of beaches — hard sand, soft sand, shale and pebble beaches and so on. Maybe I'll just hop from place to place and as I do that, one of the pre-requisites is staying in a place that's on the beach by the sea. This isn't about the how of anything, it's about the what and where.

Finally, we have the Experience quadrant. What are the experiences you want to have in your life? The type of things that may be a one-time only deal like climbing Everest, trekking through the Amazon, doing the

Orient Express train journey across Europe, or going into space. These are the things you would want to experience if time, money, or location was not a concern.

The good thing about this quadrant is that these experiences can be as fanciful as you want. And I know what you are thinking — you are thinking, what's the point of writing unrealistic things? Who says they are unrealistic? You might not be able to experience them right this second but who says you can't in 5, 10, or 20 years?

The whole purpose of this exercise is to create a vision for your future so you know what you are working towards.

Another person I supported with their TALE Grid wrote down that they wanted to spend a month in Japan learning the basics of being a Samurai. In the Activities quadrant, they had already written about learning martial arts of different types so this Experience was an extension for them and something they were passionate about.

I'd also like to quickly take a moment to talk about the types of things you shouldn't write down in your grid. Things like "get another degree", "move to the position of VP in the company" or "earn X per month" are what Vishen Lakhiani calls Means Goals. He talks about them in his book and that they are the type of goals where you write them in the format of "X so Y", like this: "earn X per month so I can spend the weekends doing Y". The "spend the weekends doing Y" is an End Goal in his book, the thing that's going to bring you happiness and joy, and that's the type of thing to write in your TALE Grid.

We don't need to concern ourselves with the "how" of getting to a point of being able to do these activities, spend your time, live where you want to live, or experience the things you write down. Napoleon Hill writes that the path might not be clear to us but having the burning desire for something and focusing on it with persistence can lead us there. He gives the example of Edwin Barnes who wanted to be a business partner of Thomas Edison. Barnes didn't know how he was going to achieve that but he got a job, worked his way in the Edison business at a lower level until 8 years later, saw an opportunity to help Edison promote his new dictating machine, and successfully turned himself into Edison's business partner.

Hill wrote about opportunity:

> ***"That is one of the tricks of opportunity. It has a sly habit of slipping in by the back door, and often it comes disguised in the form of misfortune, or temporary defeat."***

Worrying about the how of achieving and experiencing the things in our TALE Grid will stop us from taking action and moving forward. We also need to move away from the thinking that something is impossible. If we look through history and the moments that changed everything, if the people involved in those moments thought things were impossible the, world would be a very different place. Those involved in the Declaration of Independence. Those involved in landing a man on the moon. Those involved in going to the deepest parts of the oceans. Those who have invented technologies and machines that changed our very existence.

If we believe something is impossible, we will find a way to make sure it doesn't happen and we will sabotage ourselves, or not pursue opportunity when it comes slyly knocking at the door.

So I urge you to suspend all doubt and write the things in your grid that you truly want and that will make you happy. What you write in your TALE Grid is personal to you and nobody else needs to see it if you don't want them to. If you do choose to share it, that's entirely up to you. In the Freedom Hunters Club, we do share our TALE Grids because it enables other people to borrow things for their grids, or find people who have the same things in their quadrants and start working together to achieve them.

The point I'm trying to make is that the TALE Grid is for you and about you. It's a reference point as you continue to move forward, it's something you can come back to and update, and it's something you can look back on and see what you achieved.

And now that we have a vision for the future, let us move to the next chapter in Part 1. The chapter is about the power of mindset, beliefs and desires.

## ACTIVITY #1 – Create Your TALE Grid

*I've given you some pointers already but now it is time to write in your TALE Grid. If you've downloaded the supporting resources, you have a template to use.*

*If not, then creating the grid on a piece of A4 paper is quick and easy, just draw a line down the middle of the page, and then across the middle of the page. This will give you your 4 quadrants and then in each one, write one of the words: TIME, ACTIVITIES, LOCATION, EXPERIENCES.*

*The next step is to write down the relevant things to you in each of the quadrants by following the instructions in this chapter. How do you want to spend your time and how much time do you want to spend working? How much time with family each day? Where in the world do you want to be located? What activities do you want to do regularly? And what experiences do you want to have in your life?*

*If you are a business owner, entrepreneur, or wanting to break free of the 9-5, think about where you'd love your business to be located, whether you want team and staff activities in your grid like day trips away, and how you split your time between your business and your home life.*

*This is personal to you and the TALE Grid is something we will refer back to throughout this book so I encourage you to take a little time to create it.*

# The Power of Mindset, Beliefs and Desires

In the previous chapter, I started to talk about desire and the stories of Edison and Ford. These all come from Napoleon Hill's book 'Think and Grow Rich' where he writes about having a burning desire. That burning desire has enabled people throughout history to achieve exactly what they set their minds to.

Hill also talks about how 'thoughts become things' and if you've ever thought about a negative situation that could happen and then it suddenly becomes reality, then you've been on the other side of this. According to Hill, you've thought that negative situation into existence.

The problem with society today is that very few of us have a burning desire. Instead, we have an attitude of "yes I'd love this but if it doesn't happen, oh well, I'll just stick with what I've got". We then meander through life and accept whatever comes our way rather than making things happen.

In Vishen's book 'The Code of the Extraordinary Mind', he talks about bending reality once we've assessed and broken through the Brules of society. He positions Brules as the BS rules of society that we are taught and that become ingrained in us like getting an education, going to college, getting a job and slogging our way up the corporate ladder, and getting married and having kids. Those things are all great if that's what we truly desire, but a lot of the time we only do them because of what society has told us we "should" do, and what's right and proper.

Bending reality is about taking a step away from the Brules, questioning them and then creating our own new rules for how we want to live and operate (as long as we don't go against the philosophy of doing no harm to others). He talks about his upbringing and how the religion of his family meant he wasn't allowed to eat beef, but he saw lots of other people eating beef so questioned this rule of his society. Another point I'd like to draw from his book is about absolute truth vs. relative truth. Absolute truth is about universal things that cannot be refuted — like we can see the moon in the sky. Everybody can look up and should be able to see the moon. The absolute truth as we currently understand it is that the moon goes through cycles, we can see it changing in terms of how much we can see of it as it goes through the crescent phases and so on.

Relative truth is something that is relative to our current view of the world and the society in which we find ourselves. Not eating beef is a relative truth because there are large portions of the world's population who eat beef. Believing your sports team is the best in the world is a relative truth because fans of other teams will likely disagree with you. Other relative truths include holy days, when and how to fast, views on the best exercise regimes, whether Marvel or DC is better or Star Wars vs. Star Trek. These are all based on our current view of things, or how we've been influenced by the people and environment around us.

If we can identify the Brules in our lives, we can start to think differently and act differently. And if we have a burning desire for what we really want, it gives us something to work towards. That's one of the reasons I started this book with the TALE Grid. To give you something to visualise and work towards, while keeping it visible, so that you have a reference point that you can turn into a burning desire.

But this chapter is also about the power of mindset and beliefs.

Both of these things go hand-in-hand. If we have a negative mindset or set of beliefs about things, it impacts our ability to take uncomfortable action and move forward. If we have a positive belief and a positive mindset, we can achieve anything. I believed my body was strong enough to heal my broken neck and it did.

Tony Robbins talks about life happening to you, or life happening for you. Life happening to you is a victim mindset, in that you are giving up your power and just letting other people and situations control your experience. Life happening for you is the opposite and a more positive perspective with you gaining the power to choose your direction, the actions you take, and having the ability to explore options.

When I interviewed Zai Miztiq for the Unchained podcast, she talked about whether we want to be a victim or be victorious in our lives. And this was coming from a lady who was in a major car accident, broke her spine and had to have rods and screws inserted into her back before learning to walk again. She used that experience as fuel to make changes and work to help other people. She's now focused on human empowerment, hosts seminars, and has written several books.

Having been an entrepreneur since the age of 16, I've faced many ups and downs, including closing 2 businesses, but I've always maintained a sense of looking through the lens of possibilities and opportunities. When we ask ourselves "what if", we can either choose to give in to the negative responses or we can look at the potential upside. Now don't get me wrong, there have been times where I've been stuck in that negative mindset until I've taken a step back and reframed things.

When I closed my first business, I put it down to the financial crash in 2008/09 and clients tightening their belts. I was fresh out of university and had seen some success with projects for Intel, Telefonica and Microsoft, but the business didn't have the stability to survive. Closing the business and opening my eyes to opportunities led me to the role at EA SPORTS and all the new experiences and learning that role brought with it. If I had done a TALE Grid exercise when I was at university and written down that I wanted to go to No. 10 Downing Street, home of the UK Prime Minister, I would have had no idea how that would be possible. It might seem impossible.

But that first business enabled me to do it. There was an opportunity to consult on a project for the UK government and after a period of time, I was invited to No. 10 Downing Street to review the project's progress and findings. Through that first business, I was also invited to write a section in an edition of the Guinness Book of World Records.

From everything I've been through, including all those ups and downs, I now believe the universe has a plan for me even if I don't fully grasp that plan and am not entirely comfortable with timelines. I look back at the experiences I've had, what I've achieved, the learnings I've gained over the years and everything that has brought me to this moment in time and writing this book for you. If anything had happened differently, you wouldn't be reading this right now.

Here's a different perspective on mindset and it comes from Professor Caroline Dweck's book 'Mindset — Changing the way you think to fulfil your potential'.

## Fixed Mindset vs. Growth Mindset

I've already talked about our mindset determining our actions, or lack of action depending on whether we have a positive or negative mindset. Prof. Dweck positions things slightly differently with a view of a fixed mindset or growth mindset.

Let's do a quick test.

There are no scores involved but it's more about seeing where you are currently.

Do you believe your skills and talents are inherent and a natural gift, or do you believe that all your skills and talents are due to training and effort?

If you sided with skills and talents being inherent and a natural gift, you lean more towards a fixed mindset. If you answered that they are due to training and effort, you are leaning more towards a growth mindset.

Here's how she compares the fixed mindset and the growth mindset.

| Fixed Mindset | Growth Mindset |
|---|---|
| Success is about proving they're smart or talented and validating themselves. Failure, like getting a bad grade, losing a tournament, getting fired or getting rejected, is a setback. Fixed mindset people believe these experiences mean they aren't smart or talented. They see effort as a bad thing and a demonstration that they aren't smart or talented. | Success is about stretching themselves to learn something new and develop themselves. To them, failure is about not growing and not reaching for the things they value. It means they are fulfilling their potential and that effort is what can help make them be smart or talented. |

Her book gives examples of research on children and adults. For the children, some of the research related to putting groups of children in a fixed mindset or a growth mindset and then giving them puzzles to do or work of different sorts.

Those placed in a fixed mindset didn't want to do harder, more challenging puzzles because their mindset worried that if they couldn't do the harder puzzles, they would be seen as a failure. Instead, they opted to re-do the existing puzzles they had already mastered because it enabled them to demonstrate they could do the puzzle and were smart.

On the other side were the children put into a state of growth mindset and these children actively engaged with the harder puzzles and saw it as an opportunity to grow and develop. They felt they were getting smarter because they were attempting and figuring out how to do the harder puzzles.

Another example she gave was of students going to university and non-native English speakers being offered English classes. Those with a fixed mindset rejected the idea of learning so they didn't look "stupid" and that they needed the lessons, while those with a growth mindset gladly accepted the opportunity to improve and expand.

The same was true in business. CEOs with a fixed mindset surrounded themselves with people who worshipped their abilities and kept the business on the same path. Prof. Dweck gives Lee Iacocca of Chrysler Motors as an example and churning out the same model cars with very few tweaks or adjustments based on the changing market. And then you had CEOs with the growth mindset who went to work wanting to learn more about every aspect of the business to understand what was working, what wasn't, and how things could be improved. They didn't sit in ivory towers but got their hands dirty to move the business forward. They risked the wrath of shareholders, investors and Wall Street to set the business up for long-term growth rather than a short-term boost in the market.

It's also important to understand that in certain areas of our lives, we may have one or the other mindset. When I read this, it made a lot of sense.

Another example in the book was about learning to draw self-portraits. There was a short 5-day course and students were encouraged into a growth mindset. The before and after drawings of the students that Prof. Dweck shares in her book are amazing and highlighted that with the right focus, effort, and mindset, we can improve things.

But if we have a fixed mindset, it can be more challenging. The example of the drawing class was great for me because growing up, the story I told myself was that I wasn't good at art. My sister had all the talent (fixed mindset) but I was awesome at sport and could learn any sport really easily (growth mindset). Based on this view, I did easily pick up and play multiple sports during my school years and was selected to represent my local region at rugby. My sister was the complete opposite and put her effort into her art and learning different techniques (growth mindset) and steered away from sport because she thought she wasn't good at it and had no ability (fixed mindset).

Now, her art skills are breathtaking. She uses an art form called pointillism where there are no lines, everything is individual dots that she creates and uses those dots to build up an image. She also has the ability to create replicas of animals and objects just by looking at an original in a different art form. There's no tracing involved.

Here are some examples of her work using pointillism, although you might not be able to see all the individual dots in these (and she does accept commissions if you are interested).

*You can see above that the stag is not finished with the antlers still to be drawn*

*In these elephant drawings, the baby elephant goes from the outline of a trunk to a full trunk*

You can see more examples of Caroline's work on her Facebook page — https://www.facebook.com/CSideriusArt.

—

Another few points to add and put things into perspective before I wrap up this mini-section.

Mozart took 10 years to create anything meaningful.

Darwin spent half a lifetime researching, having conversations with others, and creating various drafts of his works.

Edison had over 30 assistants to support him and the light bulb was a series of smaller inventions that came together with constant trial and error.

Prof. Dweck writes:

> ***'Just because some people can do something with little or no training, it doesn't mean that others can't do it (and sometimes do it even better) with training.'***

If we want to break free of where we are, then the growth mindset will be an important ally in achieving this. As you read through the rest of this book, you may well identify areas where I'm talking about things that could easily fit into the category of growth mindset, especially how we can break through the knowledge chain.

## Beliefs, Emotions, and Confidence

Building from the two mindsets and suggesting that we utilise a growth mindset to move ourselves forward, I would now like to take a moment to consider beliefs.

If we fill our heads with negative beliefs, that things are impossible, and that we aren't worthy of achieving the things we want, then it's very unlikely we will achieve them. But if we reframe, look at the positives and the opportunities, and believe it's possible because others have been able to do it, we start to look at the world differently.

There was a tough period when I was writing this book after I had just finished a project. I was waiting for an invoice to be paid and had $100 to my name, but I believed there were better times ahead. That belief carried me through, even though living through the day-to-day was tough. I believed there were opportunities out there for me and I believed I could evolve the business into something that was more aligned with my core values and what I wanted to achieve.

Paul Raimon Massey, one of my podcast guests on Unchained, talked about the body as being a machine, and our brain like a hard drive. We have the ability to change our thinking and uninstall negative beliefs and views of ourselves and the world around us. Vishen echoes this in his book and talks about our operating system and that we can regularly update with new knowledge and thinking.

Meditation, gratitude practices, and affirmations are great for this re-wiring or re-coding. It's something I started doing and it has certainly helped me change my perspective on situations, who I am, and the experiences I've had. It's also important to understand our past is in the past. It happened; we can't change that. And we shouldn't let it hold us back, but we can learn from it in order to avoid the situations and experiences from repeating.

Paul started meditating and reading self-help books while he was working as a mercenary protecting ships from Somali Pirates around the Horn of Africa. He had time on his hands and so devoted it to learning and re-wiring his thinking. Now he's a mindset coach helping entrepreneurs overcome limiting beliefs so they can further grow their businesses.

Neil Dylan Young, whom I also interviewed, has a series of mantras that he constantly says to himself to shape his thinking and responses to the situations he faces every day. His change in perspective and thinking enabled him to grow an engineering consulting business to $5M in annual revenue and now he spends his time coaching others.

What we tell ourselves in our heads shapes our view of the world and the reality we live in. We have the power to change that and it's a power we were born with. It all comes down to neuroplasticity which is the ability for the brain to create new neurons and new connections. Every time we have a new experience, or start learning a new skill, neuroplasticity comes into play and changes the way our brain is structured and functions. If we keep repeating negative thoughts, those connections get stronger; if we repeat bad habits the, connection in our brain gets stronger. Which means we can also use that ability to our advantage. If we think of positive thoughts and take positive actions, practice meditation and spend time in a calm state, we reinforce the positive connections in our brain. Over time, we can literally re-wire our brain and shift from negative to positive.

But I appreciate you might be sitting there reading this and saying to yourself, "Philip, that's great but... I struggle to deal with my emotional responses to people or situations. I'd love to have a positive mindset and view of the world but my emotions always take over."

If that's you then I want you to know I hear you, and I want to offer a view through a different lens when it comes to managing emotions. I've had many ups and downs, some of which I've already written about, and I'm someone who regularly turned to food like ice cream, chocolate, and cake when I was having a bad day. I was an emotional eater.

And so, I'd like to introduce you to Clarence. Clarence is my emotional chimp that lives in my head. In Professor Steve Peter's book "The Chimp Paradox", he explains that the emotional centre of our brains, the limbic centre, is faster to work and act than the more logical part of our brains, the frontal lobe. He likens it to a chimp (emotional) and a human (logical). These are independent personalities with different agendas, ways of thinking and modes of operating.

As soon as I started to recognise Clarence was the one responding to certain situations, I was able to start managing my chimp and that's what Prof. Peters talks about in his book. The chimp in our head can be very constructive or very destructive but it is not good or bad, it is just a chimp.

Your human and chimp will do battle throughout your life and the chimp will work to keep you safe and secure. It thinks catastrophically and overreacts to situations. It's the part of you that thinks the worst and takes things out of perspective, like when you haven't received a response to a message or emails in 48 hours and you believe the world might be ending. I know, I've been there with Clarence.

The book also talks about how the chimp behaves in certain situations, like becoming anxious when they are unsure or in unfamiliar situations. The chimp asks questions like "But what if it goes wrong?" and "But what if I can't do it?".

Once we recognise these questions and thoughts are coming from the chimp inside us, we move into a position of being able to manage it. Prof. Peters writes:

> ***"Part of the problem is that most people don't realise that the chimp is merely making an offer and not a command. You do not have to follow your emotions, you have a choice."***

This realisation has certainly helped me on many occasions and enabled me to assess that internal voice and whether it's me (the logical human) or Clarence trying to kick off and cause some drama.

You may be reading this as someone who is able to switch their mindset, think positively, and take action and that's great — keep going! But if you are someone who recognises reluctance in decision-making, lots of emotional responses to people and situations, and a feeling of not being in control of your thoughts, hopefully this reframe with the chimp can help you.

I also think it's important to touch on confidence because it's attached to belief. Believing in yourself and your ability to adjust and cope with situations can give you the confidence to start. You then build confidence in your ability at a certain task or activity the more you do that task or activity, become familiar with it, and start to develop your skills and identify ways to improve.

Prof. Dweck writes:

> ***'In the growth mindset, you don't always need confidence. Even when you think you're not good at something, you can still plunge into it wholeheartedly and stick to it. Actually, sometimes you plunge into something because you're not good at it.'***

The whole reason I've written this book is to share my journey of how I've changed my mindset, reshaped my life, my recognition of the 12 chains, and to help you break free so you can live the life of freedom that you desire. Shifting mindset, having the belief in what's possible, and understanding the chains holding us back all play together. Once we understand the chains, we can reshape our beliefs and gain the confidence to overcome them which is exactly what we will be going through in Part 2 when we look at each of the 12 chains.

But first, I want to take a minor detour to talk about the difference between happiness and freedom.

# The Difference Between Happiness and Freedom

It has been written on many occasions that people who win the lottery only stay happy for a short period of time until the money fades or their gratitude for their new situation fades.

This book is all about helping you break the 12 invisible chains so you can find freedom in your life, and your view of freedom might be very different from mine. Our TALE Grids may look completely different so here's how I'd like to position happiness and freedom:

Happiness is a state of mind.

Freedom is about how we live our life on a daily basis.

We can be happy even if we haven't yet achieved the freedom we are looking for because happiness is a state of mind.

We can achieve time, money, and location freedom and still be unhappy.

I think this is an important distinction. If I refer back to the TALE Grid, this was an attempt to get you to identify the activities that increase your level of happiness while working towards the vision you have of freedom for your life. I call these activities 'Freedom Activities' precisely because they are things that make us feel good and give us a small sense of freedom — we have chosen to spend our time doing them.

As Prof. Peters writes in "The Chimp Paradox":

> ***"Happiness is a choice. Being happy all of the time is unrealistic; there will always be adversity and setback. It is natural to have ups and downs but you can get back to happiness by working on it."***

These activities and the things we want to spend our time doing can help us get back to a level of happiness. And here's a great quick and easy exercise I learned:

Close your eyes and think of a time that made you happy, that made you smile.

Picture the scene in your mind and relive the experience, the sights, the sounds, the smells.

Open your eyes.

Chances are you are smiling and feeling a little better about yourself and the world.

This demonstrates that happiness is a state of mind. By remembering and reliving a positive memory and experience that made you feel good, you gave your happiness in the here and now a little boost.

We all have the power to manage our state and it's something that Tony Robbins continually talks about and provides priming exercises to support this. He has a routine to get himself into "state" before he goes on stage so that his energy is focused on supporting the audience and showing up as the best version of himself. Other speakers do the same. Sports stars visualise their performance and get themselves into a state to perform at their best.

And we can do it too. We can take learnings from all these people and put ourselves in a position to manage our state and our state of happiness. This is important as we work towards our visions and dreams and our view of freedom.

The path to achieving the freedom we desire is likely to be winding and uncertain and if we can't manage our level of happiness, we will be less likely to take the action we need to move forward.

If we feel negative towards a situation, or are having a bad day or week, and we let that affect us so much that we stop doing things, that's like playing a board game and drawing a card that says go back 5 spaces.

We end up delaying what we really want because we aren't able to manage ourselves in the here and now.

So, what are some other considerations for happiness?

Prof. Peters writes that happiness comes at a price because it usually takes effort. But if we know that it takes effort, and there are activities, people or situations that make us feel good and improve our happiness, how much effort is actually involved?

There may be some effort in terms of travel, time, or money, but is that a price we are willing to pay for boosting our happiness for a while so that we can focus on activities and tasks that may be less exciting but will help us move towards freedom?

In my mind, that's a reasonable trade-off.

As things have come into my life to knock me off-centre, I remind myself that happiness is a state of mind and that I have the power to control it. I look for things to bring me back up and this is the perfect time to talk about energy levels. This was a model introduced to me by Ajit Nawalka.

He talks about waking up in the morning and having his battery and energy at 100%. As we go through the day, there are activities we do that will drain that battery and energy, like a job with unnecessary meetings or colleagues that do nothing but talk negatively. When we reach the end of the day, we come home and our energy is depleted and then we wonder why we might be a bit snappy or short with family and friends.

Ajit says the alternative is to build things into our day that can recharge us bit by bit. It could be taking a walk through nature at lunch time, or reading a book, or listening to music. Anything that makes us feel good can be used to give the battery a little charge boost so that at the end of the day, we don't feel as drained. For him, he has a morning routine to try and get himself to 110% charge before he starts any tasks for the day so that he has plenty of energy to give to his work and the people around him.

When we achieve freedom in our lives, we increase the potential to have this battery at a good level of charge because we will be living a life by design. A life based on how we want to spend our time, the activities we want to do, the people we want to be around and where we want to be.

On the flip side, if we can't manage our state, our energy, and our state of happiness, then achieving what we want in life will likely take longer and be much more challenging to achieve.

Seeing the negative in everything, giving into the emotions of the chimp in our head, not recognising our achievements and celebrating them, and not finding ways to make ourselves happy is like — to use a Star Wars analogy — the path to the dark side.

So, happiness is a state of mind and freedom is a way of living.

And to achieve freedom, we need to be aware of the 12 chains that hold us back which is where we are going next.

## Part 2
# The 12 Invisible Chains Holding Us Back

---

Now that we have a vision for our lives and we understand the power of mindset, beliefs and desires from Part 1, our next step is to understand the 12 invisible chains that hold us back from moving forward and living a life of freedom.

Each chain has been given its own chapter and I've done this on purpose. The chains in your life may be different from the person sitting next to you and so Part 2 can also be a dip "in and out" section — a part of the book where you can dip back in and pick out a specific chain rather than having to re-read the entire book.

The next chapters are also written in a specific order which will become clear in Part 3 when we start looking at how to break the chains.

The 12 chains are:

- Knowledge
- Speed
- Convenience
- Relationships
- Priorities
- Responsibilities
- Location
- Time
- Risk

- Fear
- Perception
- Pressure

Sadly, there's no clever phrase to remember these or the order they are in. Over time, they will become more familiar. You can turn them into a hit list and cross out the chains as you break through them because those moments are things to celebrate.

Inside the community, we encourage our "Freedom Hunters" to share those moments so that we collectively can celebrate them and their accomplishment.

And I'm not going to sugar coat things; breaking some of these chains can be hard and take time. But the fact that we know what they are means we can begin to recognise them in our daily lives, the repeated patterns or behaviours, and then start to make changes.

Some of the chains you break through may suddenly appear again as you grow and change and that's okay. If you've broken through once, you can break through again. This is what I experienced in my own life — the fear of what feedback I'd get after publishing my first book having never written one before. I broke through that chain and published the book anyway, but the fear tapped me on the shoulder again when I started thinking about launching a podcast. Regardless, I broke through and launched it because I knew it was something I needed to do for myself, and to help others.

Moving towards freedom is an ongoing process as you change and grow, and the world changes around you. Having the power to break these 12 chains will enable you to keep making progress towards your desires and your vision.

Now it's time to explore each of the 12 chains.

# CHAIN #1 — Knowledge

Knowledge may sound like a strange thing to position as a chain that holds us back, but there are two types of knowledge — the knowledge we have, and the knowledge we don't. There are three ways that knowledge can help us achieve what we dream of.

We often believe we have all the knowledge we need.

We might have a degree, might have taken some courses or watched some videos.

But for the vision of your life that you've created, I can guarantee there will be knowledge gaps that you need to fill.

If your desires for life include living on a beach or desert island, do you know the tax laws for that place? Or how easy it is to move there and the cost of living? Do you need special permits to rent or purchase property?

This is an example of the knowledge you might need for the Location part of your TALE Grid.

When I started writing my first book, I had no idea how to publish on Amazon so I had to gain that knowledge. I asked people, I looked in groups, I read the guide documentation on Amazon and then followed the steps.

I was able to fill the knowledge gap that I had for that specific thing that I wanted to do. The same was true for launching my podcast. I watched some training from John Lee Dumas, host of the Entrepreneur on Fire podcast. He provided details on a platform to use for hosting the episodes, how to create a good image for the show listing on Spotify and Apple, what to think about for episode titles and the show description and other key areas. After watching the training, I went and investigated that platform. I used the knowledge to create the show and make the episodes available on Spotify and Apple Podcasts.

*(Side note — the Unchained podcast is available on Spotify, Apple Podcasts and other platforms. The episodes are a mix of chats with special guests about the chains they've broken through and what freedom means to them, coaching sessions, and general thoughts about freedom. You can find links to each platform by going to www.finallyfindfreedom.com/podcast).*

If your vision of freedom is having your own business, ask yourself what knowledge you need to gain to start this process.

Perhaps you need to gain the knowledge of the best way to build an audience on social media. Or the knowledge of the best content strategies so you can easily create content for your audience. Or how to build a funnel and sales page to sell what you have.

Maybe you need to understand what a lead magnet is, the definition of LTV and CAC, or how to calculate profit margins. I'm not going to go into these now but hopefully, you see the point I'm trying to make. If we know where we want to get to in our lives, there's a good chance that we will need to level up our knowledge in certain areas and that knowledge will help us do one of three things — 1) move forward in something we are already doing, 2) unlock new opportunities, or 3) change our perspective on people, situations, and activities.

The knowledge we seek to gain can help us improve something we are already doing. This could be a faster way of doing X, or getting better at planning, or a new technique for Y. Not exactly rocket science but it still helps us move forward because we free up head space and potentially time.

When I created my first business straight after finishing university, I had experience in the video game industry so believed I could support brands and other clients, but I lacked some credibility because my degree wasn't in marketing, it was in computing. It also didn't help that I'd failed my first attempt at getting a degree because I failed a module twice and had to change course for my final year and only just scraped a 2:1 certification.

With the recognition of this knowledge gap, I decided to undertake a 1-year Master's in International Marketing at the same time as trying to run and grow a consulting and agency business. The course content was useful even if the delivery element was a little off — I was 1 of only 2 English people on the course at my local university. Please don't get me wrong here, I have nothing against people of different nationalities. I grew up playing video games and running teams with players from a mix of different countries and living in Dubai — you constantly come across people from all corners of the globe. Through messaging, I see claims that Dubai is home to people from over 200 different nationalities. My point is that, for this higher level of learning where a lot of it was project-based, I struggled with language barriers, ways of working and different perceptions of the world. That's on me and something I fully recognise and hold my hands up to. If I were to go back and do it all again with the knowledge I have now, I would approach the situation very differently. But at the time, being about 23 years old and trying to simultaneously grow a business meant my view of the world was very different.

But I made it through and received my Master's certification. And I had a better understanding of some of the principles of marketing and this supported me in conversations with potential clients. I had broken the knowledge chain and filled the knowledge gap to support me in an area I identified I had a gap.

The second way that new knowledge can help us is by unlocking new opportunities. Before the first edition of the Dubai Esports & Games Festival, I had no experience of using the game Minecraft Education. I was vaguely familiar with the premise of the game and how you played but I'd never spent any time looking at it.

I had a knowledge gap that I knew I needed to fill. I went and spoke to people, played the game a bit, and became more familiar. I gained enough knowledge to deliver the project and started to feel more comfortable. That new knowledge meant I could also do something new — I could have conversations with schools about running Minecraft activities in their schools for their students. This became a new opportunity for me, but it was only unlocked because I gained the knowledge and filled a gap.

Another great example is Dino, or as he's more commonly known online — the "Art of Purpose". Dino was a band director at schools in the US and during the pandemic lockdowns, he started using Twitter. Over time, he gained the knowledge of the best type of tweets to write, how to engage and grow an audience, and how to deliver value. By filling the knowledge gap, he unlocked new opportunities and built an audience of over 300K followers, created a paid community called Masterclass247, launched courses about how to write and grow on Twitter, and quit his day job of 20 years. He's also generated over $800,000 just from being on Twitter.

Eddy Quan also dived into Twitter, now X — before that, he dabbled with writing erotic fiction ebooks, providing services on Fiverr, and a few other things until he settled on Twitter and grew his audience. However, for him, the knowledge gap he filled was about email. He built his email list and now generates money each day by sending out a daily email to his audience. He's also made the decision to live in Colombia because he's been able to find his freedom and that move also meant he took it upon himself to break the knowledge chain by learning conversational Spanish.

There are countless other people who have unlocked new opportunities in their lives because they've broken the knowledge chain and gained new knowledge.

The third way that new knowledge supports us in moving forward is because of the power it has to change our perspectives on people, situations, and activities. Throughout time, there have been instances where new knowledge has helped people see things from a different perspective and take steps forward. The earth is flat vs. the earth is round is a simple example I like to use.

Another simple example is riding a bike. We can gain a basic understanding by watching but once we learn exactly how the brakes and the gears work, we now have a much better understanding of the activity that is riding a bike.

Changing our perspective on people is another thing that new knowledge gives us. We can learn about people in history, read biographies, or if we want to be more present in our current situation, we can gain knowledge of why someone reacted like they did or did something the way they did. The person speeding on the highway might not be a jerk, they might be in a rush to get to a hospital because they got a message about a loved one. But if we didn't gain the knowledge about this person and situation, we would probably continue to think they were a jerk and were putting everyone else at risk.

Knowledge is powerful and that's why lack of knowledge is a chain we need to break through. Lack of knowledge can hold us back from what we want to achieve and filling a knowledge gap can open up a whole new way of being, of operating, and of seeing the world.

### ACTIVITY #2 – Assess the Knowledge Gap

*I've just talked about breaking the knowledge chain by filling the gap in the knowledge I needed for publishing a book on Amazon. Now it's your turn.*

*Based on your TALE Grid, create a list of all the knowledge you think you'll need to support you in achieving the items in your grid.*

*If you've written down that you want to live somewhere different, think about those fun things like taxation and immigration. Think about the cost of living and visas.*

*The goal is not to overwhelm you, which I appreciate could be the case if you have a long list, but overwhelm only happens if you let it. Instead, see your list as a "to do" list and things that you can work towards and cross off. You don't need to have everything crossed off by tomorrow, but at least you now have a guiding list of the knowledge that will support you in achieving the things in your TALE Grid.*

*We will also be coming back to this list in a later chapter of the book.*

# CHAIN #2 – Speed

Speed is another chain that holds us back. The speed of thought. The speed of progress. The speed the world changes.

Technology is continuing to evolve and we are now living in a world where AI is being introduced to everything and there's a fear it will replace lots of jobs. The speed of adoption for this new technology can be as frightening as the speed at which new technology is created and brought to market. The iPhone and iPad are now common but at one point, they didn't exist. Neither did Facebook, Instagram, Twitter, or TikTok.

We sometimes struggle with the speed of change and feel that everything moves too fast.

But there's a flip side to that.

We also believe that things aren't moving fast enough.

The world has moved to a point where we expect instant gratification, growth to be instant, progress to be instant and that by doing a Thanos snap of our fingers the vision, dreams and desires we have will come to fruition.

I'm probably one of the worst culprits for expecting everything to move quickly. When I first started playing video games online with friends, I was introduced to a world that never slept, and where so much happened in the space of a week. New competitions would be announced, teams would break up and new ones would be formed, game updates would be released, events would happen, and gossip would be posted on forums and news portals. There was always so much going on and changing.

Part of me still lives in that frame of mind where I know lots of things can happen quickly, but I've also had to slow down and appreciate that some things take time.

To break through this chain, we need to realise that everything has a timeline to it, even if we don't know what that timeline is or don't like it. Completing a degree can take time. Building a business can take time. Working your way towards freedom can also take time as much as we'd love to achieve it tomorrow.

Learning a new skill is exactly the same. Malcolm Gladwell wrote that it takes 10,000 hours to master a skill but it will also take focused repetition and feedback as referenced by Prof. Caroline Dweck in her book.

When we learn a new language, we need to first understand the basics and the constructs of the language and build up to words, phrases, and conversations. When we learn a new sport, we might learn the basics of movement and how to play before learning all the different rules. I remember this from rugby — at an early age, it was about running, passing, scoring, and getting tagged. From there, more structure was put into the game with things like offside rules, proper tackles, the need to pass backwards, and which errors caused the ball to be given to your opponent. The next step up was learning the intricacies of the different rules like what happened when you kicked the ball out from certain parts of the pitch and whether it bounced before crossing the touchline.

If all this was dumped on me straight away, I wouldn't have been able to make sense of it and I'd definitely feel overwhelmed. But as I was in the moment and just enjoying playing, I wasn't thinking about what came next — I was just learning as I was going and knew that progress would come and that someone else like a coach was monitoring that progress.

The same is true for speed. Once we recognise that there will be a requirement for time to pass before we reach our vision and desires, it becomes easier to live in the present. We definitely need to keep one eye on what we want to achieve to make sure we don't veer off course but we also need to embrace the journey because what we want isn't going to happen by tomorrow.

In the previous chapter where we talked about filling a knowledge gap, sometimes the speed of progress will be determined by the knowledge you need to gain to move you forward.

There's also the consideration for mindset and beliefs that we touched on in Part 1. The more we believe something can happen, the more likely it is we will take action to make it happen. If we don't believe something can happen, we will always be on the back foot and that will slow our progress.

To break this chain, our goal is to accept that things will take time but that we can gain knowledge to help us speed up the progress towards freedom and our goals. Which means your "activity" is to write down all the things you currently do, and those you understand you need to do to move forward towards your goals, and then spend time identifying what you could do to speed things up.

When I wanted to do some online training for parents about screen time and online safety, I thought about advertising on Facebook and other places, but I also spent some time thinking about how I could speed up the process. I realised that the schools I had been supporting all had parent communities of exactly the people I was trying to reach. To speed up the process of getting registrations for the training, I messaged all the schools I had connections with and asked them to promote the training to their parent communities. This was a simple and quick action from my side, but it massively sped up the process of getting people registered and involved.

If one of your goals is to write a book, think about how you can speed up the process of writing it. If it's to launch your own business, think about the type of business and who you want to serve as your customers, then think about where they are and how you can get access to them.

If you have a vision for your freedom that's living in a particular country, perhaps reading everything about the country, understanding the process, and then going on holiday or vacation to that country is something that will help you speed up your progress to moving there.

We need to become comfortable with variable speeds and that speed is a chain we may regularly need to break through again and again. As long as we keep taking steps forward, and our eyes open for opportunities and ways to speed things up, we will reach the destination.

# CHAIN #3 — Convenience

Convenience is everywhere in the world today.

We have the ability to get next-day delivery on large items, almost instant delivery on food, on-demand entertainment, home check-in for our luggage before we fly and so much more.

This easy access is one of the biggest chains we need to break in our lives.

We fall into the trap of saying yes to one more episode and one more slice and I've been guilty of this on more than one occasion — I love a slice of a good chocolate cake.

But as we say yes to these things, we are saying no to something else.

We say no to having 45 minutes to learn something new when we say yes to watching another episode.

We say no to the vision we have for our body when we say yes to another slice of cake or pizza.

If we want to move towards the vision we have for ourselves, we need to break this cycle.

It starts with recognising the bad habits we have or the actions we take that are moving us away from where we want to be.

We all have the ability to say no, it's just easier to say yes and go with the flow because it's the path of least resistance. When you say no to another episode and gain back some time, you then have to decide what to do instead and how to use that time.

When I was providing training and guidance to parents about managing their child's screentime on devices, one of the key points was about the void left when device time was over. Parents needed to have something for their children to move into when device and screen time ended. Otherwise, their child would be left sitting wondering what to do next.

The same is true for us. Services like Netflix help fill the void and make it easy for us to keep going. Don't get me wrong, some series I've watched have been really enthralling, but I also know that's been time that I could have spent doing something else.

If I look back at the time I've spent playing video games over the years, partly because it's an industry I worked in, partly because I enjoy playing them and working through a challenge and story, I've easily spent over ten thousand hours playing them. I've played every game in a particular game franchise since it was launched 15 years ago and because of the style of game, I can easily sink 70-100 hours in each new version. For easy maths, that could be 1,000 hours on a single-game franchise over the past 15 years.

It was easy for me to grab the next new title and spend time playing through it because the world and universe were familiar. I enjoyed the style of game, the new version often continued an underlying story from a previous version and so I gave in to convenience over and over again.

I've since cut back dramatically, but there are still times when I like to escape into the magical worlds. Now, I'm making a conscious decision about how and when to spend my time playing.

Once we've identified the habits we have, or when we take the convenient options, we need to also understand what triggers our actions. Have we had a hard day at work and we've got no energy left so take the path of least resistance? Maybe it's because we had a really stressful encounter and feel like we need a "pick me up".

The problem with this thinking is that it is a vicious circle — the more you do it, the more it becomes your comfort zone. You then repeat the actions because we like to stay in our comfort zones where it's nice and warm and familiar.

If we can identify the habits and convenient options we take then we start to regain power. The power to take different actions. The power to make changes.

I've heard it from Dean Graziosi on many occasions and he talks about making a millimetre shift — if we take a millimetre shift today there doesn't seem to be much difference but if we keep walking that path in a year, or 2 years, we won't even be able to see where we started from or our old selves.

I mentioned the void that can be left when we start saying no to things. This is your opportunity to pursue something on your TALE Grid or to fill in a knowledge gap that you've already identified needs filling. If you gained back 1 hour per week, what could you learn or what could you do over the period of a year?

If you want to start a business and move away from the 9-5, perhaps this extra 1 hour is the perfect time to start planning, doing market research, having conversations with people, refining your offer, and starting to build your dream on the side.

If you want to move country, maybe this extra 1 hour could be used to gain the knowledge about immigration and tax laws, find and have conversations with existing residents, contact local authorities, understand the types of properties that are available, plan a visit so you know what to expect. And I'm sure there's a long list of other things related to moving to a different country that you could use the extra time for.

If a part of your TALE Grid is about contribution, could you use the extra hour a week to volunteer, help at a shelter, coach a kid's sports team, or create a course?

As human beings, we have the ability to learn and do anything. I've already talked about the example of people learning to draw in Prof. Dweck's book 'Mindset — Changing the way you think to fulfil your potential', and how, through a week-long process of teaching and practice, the students were able to dramatically improve the self-portraits they could create. They were put into a state of having a growth mindset and believing they could.

I also want to briefly talk about the power of words. The word "should" is dangerous because it leads us to feel guilty. I "should" do this, I "should" do that. We feel there's an action we need to take but we are reluctant to take it because there's something we want to do instead.

I "should" go to the gym but the new season has just been released on Netflix. I "should" eat more healthily but that chocolate cake looks so good.

If we can turn the "should" into a "will" or "will not", we can start to recondition our brain. Over time, the "will not" can become "don't" and that's what happened to me with alcohol. My internal and external statement now is I "don't" drink alcohol.

When we say we "will" do something, we are more likely to take the action we are talking about and over time, that can turn into a "must" and then the feeling that we "get" to do something. We change our comfort zone and the changes we made become more familiar and we start to enjoy the process.

Just imagine learning a new language. You have a vision for living in a different country and want to learn the language. You had the "I should learn the language" statement and then you changed it to "I will learn the language" and used your extra hour a week to take some online classes. As you became more confident with the language your statement became "I get to practice the language", and you looked forward to those sessions because you were continuing to develop a new skill and moving towards your goal.

If we continue to fall into the trap of convenience, we will look back at our life and be full of regret. I don't want that for my life, and I'm sure you don't want that for yours. Now is the time to start taking action and that starts with keeping a log of our time.

## ACTIVITY #3 – 7-Day Activity Log

*This activity is about helping you identify where you currently fall into the trap of convenience. I know it can be scary to create something that slaps you in the face and tells you that you might be wasting time, but the first step for making a change is to assess where we are currently.*

*If we can identify the activities we spend time on, and have it in black and white, it becomes easier to start making a change.*

*For a 7-day period, write down every activity you do during the day and how much time you spend on it. This should include meal-times, work, sleeping, walking the dog, watching Netflix, playing with the kids, basically anything you do.*

*If you are a business owner, or entrepreneur, also write down the different types of meetings you have and how much time you spend on them. These could be daily stand-up meetings, sales meetings, appraisals, or any other type of meeting.*

*One of the things I wish I'd done a long time ago was start to log the time I spent writing proposals and presentations that went nowhere. I could have spent that time focusing on something else to grow my business in a different way.*

*If you've downloaded the extra resource pack, you will have seen a sheet to act as your activity log. If not, then you can use an A4 piece of paper and draw 7 columns with a label for each day of the week. Then write in each column the activities you do each day and, in a bracket or circle, next to each activity, how much time you spent doing that activity.*

*Like the list of knowledge we've identified we need to gain, this activity log is something we'll come back to in a later chapter when we start looking at how to break the chains.*

# CHAIN #4 — Relationships

When I talk to people about the 12 chains, they often question this one about relationships because they create a vision of what I mean by relationships. In reality, it is all types of relationships but friendships, romantic relationships, and business relationships are the main ones I'm referring to.

First, I want to talk about the two levels of relationships, and then I want to touch on our own personal vision and the impact of relationships.

Relationships operate on two frequencies — there are those relationships that fuel us and those are people we enjoy being around. We feel alive when we are with those people, we are on the same wavelength and everything seems easy. The other frequency of relationships are the ones that drain you, fill you with dread, and you'd really prefer not to spend time with those people or in those situations.

It is easiest to think about this on a spectrum — fuelling on one end and draining on the other end. Every relationship we have will fit somewhere on this spectrum based on how the relationship makes us feel.

And sometimes the relationships will change over time, and they will move position on the spectrum. This happens as we change, as the other person changes, and the situations in our lives change. There's a natural shift that occurs and so sometimes our paths diverge, and people drop in and drop out of our lives. But the key point is that whenever a relationship drops into a negative frequency, it's important for us to re-assess the relationship and whether we want to continue feeling drained.

The vision we have for our life and how we want to live it may include some people, and it may exclude others, and that's okay. There will always be people who support you, and there are those who are in a different life story and so don't fully understand what you are aiming for and the changes you are making in your own life. There are also those who are focused on their own life, their own story, and if that's a negative story they are telling then they may be rolling that negative energy outwards, and that's what you notice from them. This may be why they sit in your spectrum in the negative area.

I've had this in business several times. A client relationship that drained me. Every time the phone rang, and I could see the caller ID, in my head I would be like "*oh no, what now?*". Once I recognised this pattern, I made a conscious decision to start moving away from the relationship because I didn't want to feel like that or be in that situation any longer. After moving away from that business relationship, I felt like a weight had been lifted. I'm not going to lie though, it was tough. This was a client relationship with one of my biggest clients at the time, but I knew if I didn't make a change, it would continue to drain me and make me feel miserable.

Shane, one of my coaching colleagues, had to make a tough decision about a romantic relationship. He was working in construction, drinking all the time, doing drugs, and partying at the weekends until one day, he decided he wanted something different from his life. He wanted to evolve and get out of that rut. His use of time changed, and he focused on learning to be a coach, the models for success, and growing a business. When he started gaining traction with his new project, he had to have a tough conversation. Shane wanted to move to Thailand and be based in South East Asia, but his girlfriend at the time wasn't ready to make that move. The energy started to turn a little negative and so Shane made the hard decision; he ended the relationship and moved to Thailand to continue focusing on his new business.

I had a similar experience when I moved to Guildford for the role at EA SPORTS in 2009. At the time, I was dating a girl and we had been together for about 3 months. When I moved down to Guildford, which is about a 2-and-a-half-hour drive from where I was previously, she would drive down almost every weekend to stay with me so we could spend some time together. Her family and main focus was up North where I'd previously been living while my focus was starting to be on my new location in the South. This continued for a couple of months until I became uneasy with the situation. I was working Monday to Friday and then most of the weekends were spent with her, which were great in their own way, but I felt like I wasn't settling into the new season of my life in Guildford.

As I continued to change and view my life through a Guildford-centred lens, I reached a point where I wanted to explore using my time for clubs and activities close to Guildford. I made the tough decision.

I explained to this girl that I needed to end things because I felt like I wasn't settling into my new life in Guildford. She was naturally disappointed and we had an amicable conversation about it. Thankfully, neither of us was the type to shout and scream about things. She left and I never saw her again.

In several of his podcast episodes, Master Coach Ajit Nawalka, founder of Evercoach, talks about his experience of relationships that drained him. He used to host parties for friends and acquaintances at the weekend. There would be times when he was talking to someone really interesting and he felt fuelled. He didn't want the conversation to end and may have been the last person wanting the party to end. And then he mentioned about other times when certain people would leave him feeling drained. Ultimately, he reached a point where he made the decision to stop inviting certain people who drained him.

There was another tough situation that I went through during COVID. My partner's friend lost their job and needed somewhere to stay while they searched for a new one. We had a spare room in the apartment and so said they could stay. What we thought would be 1-2 months turned into 6 months and while that might not sound too bad, let me go into a few more details. And please don't get me wrong, I'm not saying this friend was a bad person — far from it — but their view of the world was a mismatch to mine.

They had asthma and so felt strongly that they were in the vulnerable category for getting COVID. This worried them. They would wash all the food shopping in bleach when they got it delivered. They would rarely leave the apartment and come in contact with other people outside of going to work and doing what they needed to do. They would wear gloves and masks all the time. Now I know in a lot of countries this was mandatory but, in Dubai, at the time I'm talking about, things had started to be more relaxed. This behaviour, over a period of time, and this person's general negative outlook on the situation started to drain me. I'm not sure it was the full catalyst for their moving out but when I got COVID for the second time, from having a booster jab, they shut themselves in their room and didn't come out except to get food. And ironically, the first time I got COVID, it was after my partner and I had been out for dinner with this friend.

Once they had moved out, and there were even fewer restrictions in Dubai, I made the decision that I needed some space from this person. My partner knew how tough it had been on me during those 6 months and how drained I was with the whole situation. Whenever she went to meet her friend, she recognised that I wasn't yet ready to spend time and energy around this person.

Since then, we have been out for a few lunches and dinners before this friend moved back to the UK.

A quick side note about COVID situations. When my dad came out on holiday to visit in February 2022, he got COVID again and got locked up in his hotel room for 10 days as part of the quarantine process. My mum flew back to the UK without him. I think he lasted 4 days in the hotel because it was driving him crazy. I picked him up and drove him to ours and let him stay in our extra room so that he didn't feel like he was a prisoner. He joined us for meals but sat on the opposite end of the sofa when watching TV or reading a book. This was the period after I'd had 2 booster jabs and had COVID twice. Finally, after getting the required negative test results, he flew back to the UK.

Throughout the whole COVID period, my partner seemed like she was in a bubble. She worked in a school and was around kids every day. And when I got COVID twice, I didn't move to another room so she was constantly around me and sleeping in the same bed. I'm forever grateful for her support and resilience.

Relationships can be really tough. We feel an emotional connection and often a responsibility, which is another chain we will talk about later on. I made the decision to support my dad, but I've also made the decision to distance myself from other people and relationships.

If we don't make these tough decisions, if we don't retake our power, the power we were born with, then nothing in our lives will change. The feelings we have towards relationships can be one of the biggest things that holds us back from progressing towards the visions and dreams we have for our life.

## ACTIVITY #4 – Assessing Our Relationships

*For this activity, there's also a premade sheet in the downloadable resource pack. If you haven't got it, then take another piece of paper and write down all the names of the people you spend 2 or more hours with each month.*

*This includes people you work with and if you are a business owner or entrepreneur, this can include employees, business partners, and clients.*

*Once you have your list, I want you to score each person on a scale of 1 to 10. A score of 1 is really negative and draining while a score of 10 is a relationship and person that fuels you and brings you joy.*

*Now we can see if there are any patterns — like groups of people at work or in the office, family members, or friends who either drain or fuel us.*

*Like the previous activities, this is a list we will keep for later so don't lose it.*

# CHAIN #5 – Priorities

Chain #5 is all about Priorities. The importance we place on tasks and activities. But the problem is that as human beings, we often place emphasis on the wrong things. We choose to prioritise things that might be quick or easy to accomplish so that we feel good and that we are making progress, rather than working on the harder things that may take longer but will move us further along the path to our vision and freedom.

I've been guilty of this. I love creating "to do" lists and crossing things off and feel like I'm making great progress, but sometimes I take a step back and realise I've been prioritising the wrong things.

And the bigger priorities may have multiple steps to them that we need to work through first before we can make meaningful progress. When I talk to people about this, and in my content, the story I tell is about slaying the biggest dragon last. I'm not going to tell that story again here but I'll give you a parallel.

Growing up and playing video games meant there would normally be a story with a big baddy to defeat at the end, and on the way, you might have to do missions and quests to improve your character, equipment, and abilities. If you ran straight to try and defeat the big baddy, you would get immediately stomped on and lose the game. This happened to me on more than one occasion and so I'd run away and do all the other things to improve my character and move along the story.

This is the equivalent of trying to slay the big dragon first. Instead, we need to prioritise the little steps on the path that will lead us to the big step and have the ability to slay the big dragon.

It is important for us to assess each of our priorities and whether they are just quick wins to make us feel good or whether they are the necessary steps on the path to progress.

There is also another part to this chain that I feel is important to touch on.

There are two types of priorities.

1) The things we give priority to through an internal decision process
2) The tasks given to us by other people that we let become a priority

Type 1 is what I've just spoken about above so let us explore type 2 — the tasks given to us by other people.

If a task is given to us by someone else by default, it is not a priority for us. Otherwise, it would already be on our priority list. It's actually a priority of the other person and they are hoping to make it one of our priorities. The easiest example of this is when your boss gives you a last-minute task just before you plan to head out of the office. You weren't even aware of it so it wasn't on your priority list but it's on your boss's priority list and so they are trying to make it your priority.

Sadly, my partner would get this all the time from the school she worked at. Requests would be put out for all staff members to complete X, Y, and Z before the end of the school day even though the day was full with teaching, covering other classes, marking, meetings, and planning for the next day.

To break through this chain, we need to constantly ask questions about the tasks on our "to do" list and whether they are a priority that we've created, or a priority of someone else that has been handed to us.

The more things on our list that have been given to us by others — and we've turned into one of our priorities — the slower our progress will be towards our vision and the freedom we are looking for. We need to find a way to stop accepting tasks or requests that don't support us, and I appreciate this can be tough. That's why it's a chain that holds us back.

We can take the first step by doing an assessment of priorities and identifying which are those that have been given to us. Then we can work to understand if there are repeated patterns. For example, every time on a Friday afternoon, the boss comes with a request. If that's a repeated pattern, consider ways to negate this pattern — can you build it into your workflow and present your boss with the report before they ask for it? The difference in this situation is that you've chosen to prioritise this task or activity ahead of time and have more control over it, rather than it being something that's passed on to you with an expectation that it becomes your priority.

One of the main things that used to frustrate me was meetings about meetings. They didn't really serve a purpose and were a waste of everyone's time. I'm sure you've had similar situations in your life where you stand there and silently ask whether there's any point to this meeting or appointment. I've also been in that situation of getting requests for reports and sometimes I look at the type of report that's being requested. In my view, it's a silly request because I've been given no context as to why it's important.

These last-minute requests, and the expectation from others that the things or tasks they give us become our priority, are a path to frustration and eventually burnout.

Another way to manage these situations is to understand timeframes. How long will something take you and how long do you have to complete it? If you can manage or finesse expectations about when you will be able to complete a task based on current workload and other priorities (including your own), you can give yourself some extra breathing room. This is something I do when I'm asked the question "when can you do this by?". This is the question I love because it gives me some flexibility to think about my priorities and where I can fit in this other person's priority. Sometimes, if I've been pitching for business and the question from a potential client is "when can you send me a proposal by?" I might prioritise this a little higher because it is a potential opportunity for me to secure new business or an extra project.

The tougher situation is when you are told a hard deadline like "I need this by 4 pm today". In this case, we need to seek clarity on how important this task is. My normal response would be something along the lines of "thanks for letting me know. Just so I'm clear, how does this rank against X, Y, and Z as I won't be able to get all of those done today if you want me to focus on this new thing?". This gives the other person the opportunity to help you understand which things to focus on and which things to drop, or they might even drop the very thing they just asked you to do by 4 pm because they made the decision that the other items are more important.

Like all the chains that hold us back, this can take some time and effort but if we recognise the chain, and these situations in our life, we can begin the work to break them.

## ACTIVITY #5 – Assessing Our Priorities

*This chapter has looked at the two different types of priorities and so this activity is about writing them down.*

*The downloadable resource has a sheet split into 2 with a column for you to write your own priorities and the things you deem are important. The second column is for those activities and "priorities" given to you by other people that aren't actually your priorities.*

*This can be a little tricky because we often accept other people's priorities as our own, but if we look deep down and ask the question "which would I rather do?" you will be able to identify your own priorities and those given to you by other people. You can also do it by asking the question of where did the priority originate from — you or someone else.*

*If you haven't yet downloaded the resource pack, you can get it at www.finallyfindfreedom.com/resources.*

# CHAIN #6 – Responsibilities

In the chapter for Chain #5 about Priorities, we looked at the two different types of priorities — those we decide, and those tasks or things given to us by other people in the hope they will become our priorities.

The same is true with responsibilities — there are two types.

1) Responsibilities that we want or willingly take on
2) Responsibilities given to us by others, often without consultation, or that we feel obliged to take on

The first type of responsibility is the positive type. If we have actively chosen a responsibility because it fits our skillset, desires, or view of the world at that moment in time, it becomes less of a burden to us, at least in the beginning. We become enthused with the new responsibility and put the time and effort into completing it.

Putting yourself forward to help coach your child's sports team, helping at the community centre, or taking on responsibility for collecting and delivering things are simple examples of responsibilities that people willingly take on.

Throughout my life, I've constantly taken on the responsibility of creating and growing a project or a business. I've been an entrepreneur since the age of 16. In the early years, it was gaming teams and event brands. Then it was consultancy companies. Then tech platforms and mobile apps. Then educational activities for schools and students. Some were successful, others less so, but these were responsibilities I wanted and chose to take on.

However, it's also important to understand that over time, our view of the world may change, and our priorities may change. What was a responsibility we willingly took on and initially enjoyed could also become something that we feel holds us back if we want the time and energy to focus on other things.

This was the case when I was working at EA SPORTS on the FIFA video game between 2009 and 2011. I had an amazing 18 months and was involved in managing the community of players of the game in the UK. I had responsibility for a user forum with over 200,000 players in it which I managed with a small team. I had the opportunity to host events, go to football matches at Wembley, create an early version of EA's influencer program, and several other things.

But the role I was in was a contract role which meant I could only work 11 months out of 12, and it looked unlikely that the role would be made permanent which meant there was no growth opportunity for me. So as the responsibility and situation in my mind started to turn negative, I started looking for other roles. I moved to a 6-month contract at Disney that had the potential to become permanent. In reality, the role that I left at EA SPORTS did eventually become a permanent role, and the person I brought in to replace me was the one who became fully employed. And I could look back on this with frustration but, if I had stayed and the role had become permanent, then I would not have done any of the other things in my life since that point in 2011.

It's a careful balancing act, but when the responsibilities we wanted, or took on willingly, start to become negative, we need to make changes.

And the second type of responsibility is the one I see as having the potential to be more negative. The ones that have the potential to quickly sour us when left to fester. As human beings, we often don't like being told what to do unless we can see the positive reasoning behind it or have had some involvement in creating the decision or the responsibility.

If we are just handed a new responsibility without any consultation and it sits against our values, view of the world, or our goals, we will be quick to rebel against it.

With lots of my friends in Dubai being teachers, I've seen this on several occasions. Classroom teachers are offered the "opportunity" to take on responsibility for a middle leader position, like a head of a subject, that will require extra time, commitment, and effort, but without any extra pay. The school wants this teacher to have the responsibility for the subject because they need someone in that position but often won't provide the support that's required by the teacher to do those new tasks to the best of their ability.

For teachers who accept this responsibility, it can quickly turn into a negative as they get weighed down by the extra work and lack of support until they make the decision to hand back responsibility for this "new and exciting" role.

To break through this chain, we need to assess each of the responsibilities we have and decide if they are ones we want, or are ones that fall into the second category, the negative category.

Once we've identified the responsibilities we have in the second category, we can assess them further — which ones are responsibilities we originally wanted but now don't fit our view of the world or our priorities, and which responsibilities were handed to us by other people without our full buy-in.

There will likely be some tough conversations with people in both cases once you've made the decision to make changes to your list of responsibilities, but you will have the opportunity to frame them in different ways.

For the responsibilities you wanted to take on, you can make the case that your situation has changed and that unfortunately, you don't have the time anymore because there are other priorities in your life. And for the responsibilities handed to you by someone else, you may need to thank them for the opportunity and tell them that after careful assessment of the situation, this is not something you are able to support them with any longer, or words to that effect.

The key here is that in both scenarios, you are outlining that you've made a decision and that things need to change. You may initially feel like you are letting people down, but they will be able to find someone else to fill the gap, or change the responsibility to be more appealing to future holders of that responsibility.

I can't stress enough how negative responsibilities have the power to hold us down, drown us, frustrate us, and cause depression. If we let things get to that stage, it becomes tougher to break through any of the chains as we can enter a downward spiral.

My goal is to help you avoid this situation and gain back your power, claim back your time, and free yourself of these chains.

## ACTIVITY #6 – Assessing Your Responsibilities

*Much like Activity #5, this activity is about creating the comparison between those responsibilities you wanted, requested, and willingly took on versus those responsibilities that were handed to you.*

*Using the downloadable sheet, write in each of the columns which responsibilities you have that you wanted and are still happy to do, and which were given to you or you no longer want to do.*

*If you don't have the downloadable resource pack, then writing two columns on a piece of paper will work just as well. You can label the columns "Positive" and "Negative" to denote the two different types of responsibilities we are talking about.*

*Keep these lists safe with all your scribbles from the other activities as we will be coming back to them.*

# CHAIN #7 — Time

What is time? That's the question I asked myself when I started to write this chapter. We all have the same 24 hours in a day, but those 24 hours are just a construct, something to help us understand the world around us.

There's always been the rising and setting of the sun and, throughout history, that was our guide for when to do certain things. That all changed when we created a framework for what time was, and then developed the ability to tell the time and monitor the passage of it.

Nowadays, we are driven by alarms in the morning, scheduled meetings at specific times, and the constant game of clock-watching until we can leave or stop doing an activity.

But for this chapter, I want to look at how we use time both positively and negatively. Time is a resource just like water or money. If we use it wisely, we can achieve great things but, if we use it poorly, it can disappear in the blink of an eye.

And that's why it becomes one of the chains that holds us back from achieving what we want in life.

We allocate time to activities (and people) that do not move us forward towards our goals. In the previous chapter, I wrote about priorities, both ours and those of other people, and each of those priorities will require an amount of time to complete them.

In our minds, we create the belief that time is never-ending and we can start tomorrow, or the day after. To some extent, this is true; time itself is unending, but our time is finite and limited.

I realised this when I broke my neck. If the injury had been any worse, my time might have been over, and I could have been laid on that rugby pitch as a hollow shell with the life drained out of me.

After dealing with the aftermath of the injury, and coming to terms with the situation, I knew I had to make changes in my life and make better use of my time.

Now don't get me wrong, I still don't use time in the best way for every single second, but I've put more focus on the things that are important to me and the things I want to achieve. This book that you are reading right now is my second — the first was launched at the end of 2022. The draft version of this book in your hand was written in 6 weeks because I put the focus on it and gave myself the time to write it.

So, what's the point I'm trying to make here and how is time a chain that holds us back? Really, it's about our use of time. Patterson's Law states that an activity will expand to fill the time that you provide it, and why productivity books like James Clear's Atomic Habits and Nir Eyal's Indistractable give guidance on how to manage this situation.

James Clear talks through the process of creating new and good habits, and breaking bad habits. We all have things that we do automatically, like brushing our teeth or tying our shoes, and these are habits that have been created because we've repeated a set of actions over and over again.

And we all have some bad habits that either impact us or others, like not clearing out the sink of all the muck after washing the dishes (I was guilty of this until my better half pointed it out and told me it really annoyed her), or leaving the toilet seat up, or not putting things away and leaving the place untidy. These might be classed as low-level misdemeanours but, over time, the frustration of the person on the receiving end can build up until boiling point.

James writes that compounding bad habits and poor decisions day after day can lead to toxic results. To borrow directly from his book — 'Your outcomes are a lagging measure of your habits. You get what you repeat.'

If we have a habit of flopping on the sofa at the end of a tough day and spending 5 hours watching Netflix, that habit will form a vicious cycle — we'll feel like we're not making any progress in life because our habits are working against us. We repeat the action and so we get the same outcome. As Einstein put it with his definition of insanity — we repeat the same action and expect a different outcome. I don't know about you but if I watch 5 hours of Netflix a night, it's very unlikely I'll achieve the vision I'm looking for, because my time will mostly be split between work and Netflix with no space for activities that move me forward, or time for new learning.

In the book Atomic Habits, you are taken through a journey of how habits form, how they impact us, and what to do about them. I'm not going to drill into all the details here, but there is a thought that I do want to pull out in reference to breaking the chain of time.

A 1% improvement.

Habits can help automate our actions and behaviours, which can be really useful, and speed up things so we free up time and focus for more meaningful tasks, but what we should be aiming for on the back of creating supporting habits is a 1% improvement.

If we can achieve a 1% improvement in key areas, we will achieve an amazing level of growth over time. This is the power of compounding effort. If we commit to reading 1 page a day, that's noble. If we begin with 1 and over time, we read 2 pages, and then 3 pages, eventually we will be gaining new knowledge or experiences faster to help us break the knowledge chain.

I attempted this 1% compounding myself. I set myself the challenge of recording a 2-minute video every day for a year and posting it on my social channels. The messages varied depending on what was happening in my life at the time, or thoughts that came to me, or what I'd read. That 2-minute exercise, plus the time it took to write a caption and upload, enabled me to improve over time.

It also had a compounding effect — I was posting the videos to my YouTube channel and other places which meant they were permanently available for other people to watch, comment on, and enjoy. At first, the views trickled in, but with a little support, those daily videos started to gain traction and the compounding began — more views, more comments, and more subscribers.

All I was doing was a 2-minute video a day and posting it.

This became a habit for me because I repeated the action every day. After a while, I was asked by those around me if I'd yet recorded my video for the day and what topic I'd chosen. As James wrote in his book — 'All big things come from small beginnings. The seed of every habit is a single, small decision.'

We are all capable of making single, small decisions but what we need to do is make single, small positive decisions that move us forward, or have the ability to compound into something meaningful that moves us closer to our vision.

And you might be reading this and saying, "Yeah but Philip, new habits are so hard to stick to." And my guidance would be to read James' book because he explains in detail how to structure and design your habits so that they do stick.

Where James writes about habits, Nir Eyal writes about distraction and how our distraction comes from our dissatisfaction. In an early section of his book, he states, "In the future, there will be two kinds of people in the world; those who let their attention and lives be controlled and coerced by others, and those who proudly call themselves 'indistractable'."

We seek out distraction because we want to change our state and our emotional level. If a task is boring or frustrating, we will seek out something more pleasurable, even if that's a quick scroll on social media without a real purpose. Having the phone close by acts as a trigger and so our hand reaches for it and we load up our favourite social media app and smile at the cat or goat videos. This flow of actions — from feeling frustrated to picking up the phone to loading the app and scrolling just changed our state and emotional level.

But triggers can work against us and that is part of what Nir writes about. He gives the story of the dangers of a pedometer and how notifications about streaks and bonuses, limited-time offers, and notifications about likes and comments on social posts can turn us into zombies; relentlessly pursuing and responding to triggers.

While some people place the blame on the smartphone or device, here's what Nir has to say about it — 'Solely blaming a smartphone for causing distraction is just as flawed as blaming the pedometer for making someone climb too many stairs.'

We have the ability to control our focus and whether we let ourselves fall into the trap of triggers and distraction, so it's important to use that control to become more focused on how we use our time, especially if we want to find freedom in our lives. Endless scrolling, extra episodes, unnecessary video game time, gossip and general procrastination should be regularly reviewed under the lens of "is this moving me forward?".

I've been guilty of this throughout my life and, in some senses, I still am. My go-to activity for unwinding and switching focus was playing video games. It was mental stimulation for me because I may have been solving puzzles, exploring a story, or working out how to defeat a big baddy. I've also spent lots of time watching episodes and binging a whole series on Netflix if it's really good. There are hours here that I could have spent doing something else instead, so now I make a concerted effort to ask myself this question on a regular basis:

"Is this activity and use of time moving me forward, and if not, is it a shared experience that I'm creating?"

It is rare that I will sit and actively watch a series or films on my own but sitting and watching with my partner, well that's a different story because we are creating a shared experience. The same is true with video games, we often play together and so create shared experiences of winning and losing together with rounds of high fives when we win.

There will always be times when we want to sit and do nothing, especially after an intense period, and the realisation and drive for writing this book came to me when I was sitting by the pool after completing a 3-month government project and festival.

The project was great and fulfilling, but it also wasn't the best use of my time in terms of moving me forward. It was a means to an end and so now I assess every project to understand if it is going to help me move towards my goals.

At the very start of this book, we talked about the vision you have for your life, how you want to live, and the things you want to achieve. If we can keep that in mind at all times, we gain the power to ask ourselves the tough question about using time and using it wisely.

The very act of asking this question about how we are using our time (positively or negatively) is the first step to breaking the chain. We have assessed how we are spending our time and understanding the impact that it will have on our ability to make progress.

Each chapter in this section of the book is meant to act as a nudge and a wake-up call so that we recognise the areas where we can and should make changes if we want to be different, and experience different things in life, and time plays a key role in all of that.

# CHAIN #8 — Location

Location is the eighth chain holding us back and this might sound strange, especially if we've created a vision for our lives that includes living somewhere different, but let me explain.

A lot of the time, our location is influenced by external factors, like where we need to be for a job, or where family are located.

For the role at EA SPORTS working on the FIFA video game, I needed to be in the office and so that meant moving from where I had been living around Sheffield in the UK to being around Guildford where the office was located. I actually chose to try and find somewhere in Guildford so that it was an easy walk/drive to work each day, and I took a tiny 2-bed-room apartment that was a 15-minute walk from the office.

When I moved to the UAE, I started a mobile app company that was focused on the esports and gaming industry because that was my background and linked to the vision I had at the time. I managed to get the company into a tech accelerator program which provided some support and guidance and was able to get a few clients on board from Europe and the US. Sadly, both those clients were acquired by bigger companies and they moved away from having a mobile app strategy. I was left with no clients, and I was in the wrong part of the world — the platform that I had built was relevant to the big teams and organisers in Europe and the US because the esports market was more developed. At that time in 2016, there were no big teams or events in the Middle East and so ultimately, I was in the wrong location to grow the business, and I wasn't willing to move back having just got to the UAE. I couldn't easily get face-to-face with the decision makers in Europe and the US and eventually closed the business down.

Since that time there have been other companies who have done exactly the same thing I was trying to do, and they've had more success, but I put that down to them being in Europe and the US with easier access to the core market they were targeting.

You may say my heart wasn't in it if I wasn't willing to make the move back to the UK or Europe to gain access to the clients I wanted and you'd be right — my life and experience in the UAE far outweighed the thought of moving back to the UK with no guarantee of success.

I took a lot of learnings from this experience and the things I've leaned towards since have been more independent of location — like courses, books, and coaching.

Yes, I've still done projects in and around the Gulf region because it's easy to travel between the countries, but I've also kept one eye on, and used my time, to build resources that can be used by anyone and anywhere. This is one of the reasons I created the Freedom Hunters Club, a membership community where I can support people all over the world without concern for where I'm living. The internet has made this type of business a reality and we see more course creators, authors, agency owners, and coaches taking this approach.

I've already written about Shane making the move from the UK to Thailand as he was growing his coaching business so that he was in a location that worked for him and where he felt comfortable — it was part of his vision.

When I interviewed Freddie Pullen for one of the early episodes of the Unchained podcast, he talked me through his experience of moving to Dubai. He and his wife were in a car accident in the UK that most people thought they shouldn't have walked away from. They were driving down country roads in the UK which are quite narrow and can be very windy with regular bends, giving you no visibility of what's ahead. This is the situation Freddie found himself in and someone driving the other way, on the wrong side of the road, going round the bend ended up hitting them in such a way their car was flipped into a ditch on the side of the road.

Freddie described this as a wake-up call for him and his wife Antonia. That could have been the moment where it all ended for them. Thankfully it wasn't, and that experience enabled them to question what they wanted out of life. Freddie was already doing well working in Mergers and Acquisitions and Antonia was a celebrated interior designer, but they decided it was time for a change. Their family and friends questioned the decision to move to Dubai and start a business together but as Freddie talks about on the podcast episode — his views were "why not?".

We need to question whether the location we are in is serving us in achieving our vision and our goals. Being based in the UAE, because of time zones, makes it more challenging for me to be involved with online events in the USA.

When I did an online event from Tony Robbins — Unleash the Power Within — in July 2022, the time zone differences meant I was participating from 6 pm until 6 am UAE time for 4 days straight. I think I managed the first 2 days and then for the last 2 days, I was in bed by 3 am and missed some of the content. If I had been in the USA or UK, the time zones would have been a little more favourable.

But being in the UAE has enabled my partner and I to travel to South East Asia and go scuba diving because those countries are all closer to the UAE compared with being in the UK. I've also been able to be an extra in a film with Brad Pitt that was filmed in the UAE.

I missed out on being cast for Star Trek but I was called up as a "Marine" for the Netflix film War Machine. I got kitted out in an army uniform, told where to be and when, where to stand, what to shout as a group when we heard the cue, and a host of other instructions. In one of the scenes, the extras like me were asked to all sit around in camp idly chatting before Brad Pitt's character walks up to deliver a speech to the troops. We did a number of takes but this was an opportunity to experience a film being made, how Brad got into character and delivered his lines and all the other bits involved with shooting scenes.

For another scene, we were kitted in full combat gear and had to do circuits and bumps. This involved getting into the back of a chinook helicopter, with probably 20 people sitting on two rows down the inside of the helicopter, and circling the airfield before coming into land, dropping the ramp at the back of the helicopter, and filing out in two lines and walking towards the base. The director was trying to get a shot of troops returning to base but we did probably 8 takes of this and every time, the desire was to get the shot as the helicopters were just touching down and the troops were piling out. This meant we lifted off, circled, landed, opened the ramp, and filed out.

It was a great experience and one that I would never have had if I hadn't already been in the UAE. Sadly, where I was sat and stood in the different shots meant I got edited out of the final cut but it's a memory that will stay with me forever.

There may be opportunities around the world that may help us move forward — this might be a new job with better pay that we can reinvest in building the life we want, or the opportunity to be closer to a location we want to visit.

I also want to make a quick side note about the universe having a plan. From my experiences, I now believe this. Although I was in the wrong place for my mobile app business, being in the UAE enabled me to meet my partner, and set me on the path I'm on now after breaking my neck. I had stopped playing rugby when I was still in the UK because of a shoulder injury. I'd had surgery on it, but it hadn't fully solved the problem. The warm weather in the UAE helped me overcome the niggles and so I started playing again. If I hadn't started playing again, I wouldn't have injured my neck and would still be muddling through and feeling stuck in life.

It is easy to get sucked into a life situation and not take the time to look up and see what else is out there. The world is a big place. My TALE Grid has a house on the beach in the Location quadrant. I still don't know where in the world that is but I'm excited to explore and find it.

For us to start breaking this chain of location, it is important to assess whether the location we are currently in is contributing to that vision we've created. If the answer is no, then we need to start opening our eyes and looking for places and opportunities that will support us.

# CHAIN #9 – Risk

The definition of risk is "a situation involving exposure to danger" and this is different from fear, which we will cover in the next chapter. As the definition above outlines, it's about the situation and the action of exposure. Putting ourselves or others in the way of danger.

And the challenge with this is that danger is subjective. Which means that risk is subjective. What may be a risky action to one person might be normal to another person because they have more experience.

I've been an entrepreneur since the age of 16, and that's a vocation that a lot of people see as risky because there's no guarantee of anything working, or being successful. This has been a risk I've been willing to take, so I've never really seen it as a risk; I've seen it as a way for me to live closer to the freedom I'm looking for. Yes, there have been some very tough periods throughout my life, like closing businesses down, and periods of time with no projects and no income, but I've never seen it as risky, it just "is". In my mind, that's just what entrepreneurship "is".

You could say the decision to set up my first business straight out of university was risky because I had no real business experience before that point. I had industry experience in specific areas and I understood how I could support clients and projects, but I had no experience of the process of managing a business, securing clients, and growing a business. It was a risk but I got some great experiences out of it and some useful learnings, even if I did close it down when the 2008/09 financial crisis happened.

In my earlier years at university, on a night out drinking, I miscalculated the level of risk when taking an action because as I've mentioned, risk is subjective. I was finishing a round of drinks in a bar with one friend, and the rest of our group had already left to move on to the next bar.

When the two of us walked out, we started talking about the quickest way to get to the next bar to join our other friends. My friend wanted to take the long path, but I saw there was a roundabout with an underpass that would take us on a shorter route.

If you aren't familiar with the type of road system I'm talking about, let me explain. In the UK, we have roundabouts (traffic circles). You give way to people coming from your right because of the side of the ride we drive on in the UK. In the city centre of Sheffield, there was a roundabout like this, but it was also elevated with a passage and tunnel underneath it for people to walk through and reach different parts of the city centre. The roundabout part of the road was actually a hole so you could see down from the roundabout to the underpass. There were also sloped sides down to the underpass and then a drop. I calculated that the drop wasn't too big and that going down the slope and then jumping down would make our journey to the next bar much quicker.

I miscalculated and also misjudged my landing. I sprawled on the floor and put my hands out in front of me to act as a brace and, in doing so jarred one of my wrists. For the rest of the evening, I nursed this wrist and ended up going home early because of the pain and to put some ice on it. From my perspective, the risk of jumping down to the underpass wasn't significant so I took the action. In reality, there was more risk than I anticipated.

The alcohol definitely impacted my judgement in this situation, but it also shows that we can make different assessments about risks if we want to.

So, if danger is subjective, and by default risk is also subjective, how can we reframe our thinking so that we can break through this chain?

Firstly, we can rationalise the risk. How likely is it that something will happen? When I go scuba diving, do I stop myself because there's a risk of coming face-to-face with a great white shark? No, I've investigated how likely it is that will happen and sought guidance from the local dive masters, and that assessment enabled me to make a decision.

We can weigh up all our actions on the likelihood of having a positive or negative outcome and then choose to take the action or not. When I wrote this book, was there a risk nobody would see it, read it, or like it? Absolutely, there was that risk. But there was also the possibility it could help change lives.

Risk has been a part of life since the time we were born. As a baby, we didn't understand risk and so we barrelled around, got feedback from our actions, even if sometimes that was painful, and we continued on anyway.

This is the type of mindset that can help us as we get older. The ability to continue learning, to get feedback and to keep taking actions, even when there is a chance of a negative outcome.

If we see everything through a negative lens and that every action we take has too much risk, we will never do the things we need to do in order to move forward towards freedom. We will continually be stuck in an unfulfilling life and reach that point at the end of it where we will be full of regret.

This is something I keep in my mind as I work towards my goals and vision. I've already written about the risk of launching a book and everyone hating it. Launching a podcast had a similar risk in that it could end up with nobody listening to it. But I go back to one of the early exercises I did on my personal development journey, and you may be familiar with it.

It was the eulogy exercise, the one where you have to imagine what will be said about you at your funeral. This one exercise, and asking the question about what impact I had made on the world, is one of the biggest things I credit for helping me see the world differently and for starting to make changes in my life, even when there have been risks.

We can assess each of the risks in front of us and then take appropriate action to mitigate the risk as much as we can, or, continue to move forward with the knowledge that there is an associated risk.

Everyone's appetite for risk is different, but as I'm sure you've heard the saying before — no risk, no reward — sometimes we need to take the risky action for us to progress.

# CHAIN #10 – Fear

Fear is an interesting topic for me. I like to think I've been able to defeat fear as if fear was some shadow beast that creeps around, all-knowing but unseen, and ready to pounce on you when you least expect it. A bit like The Nothing in the film Neverending Story, which is a film I grew up adoring and loved to see the references to, and hear the soundtrack, in Stranger Things.

And the more I thought about fear, the more I realised it was just the mental image we paint inside our heads of the things that might happen to us or someone else. Because we are creative beings, this mental image is normally taken to the absolute extreme which is what causes the anxiety, the apprehension, and the reluctance to take action.

Throughout various surveys and studies, the biggest fear of people collectively is public speaking. That's not because of the act of getting on stage and speaking, which is literally just that, an act. It's the image we paint in our heads of the potential negative reaction from the audience. Are we going to get laughed at? Are we going to get heckled? Will people fall asleep when I'm talking?

This was something I myself had to deal with. In another life and another time, I used to get up in front of an audience every month and give a short talk about social media management to marketers as they were also hearing sessions about email marketing, campaign strategy, and marketing automation (like those automated sequences you get when you sign up to a new newsletter or community bulletin). I was always nervous because I was talking to marketers who might already know the information I was going to share. After doing this for maybe 8-10 months, I left the company to pursue other opportunities but I didn't get back up on stage for years. I'd pushed through and done it because it was part of the job but not something I'd really wanted to do.

More recently, after the injury and the personal development journey, when I was delivering the project for the Dubai Esports & Games Festival in May and June 2023, one of the project elements was career talks to students in schools across Dubai. I'd already decided that to help me get a message out, I needed to become more comfortable being in front of an audience and speaking on stage. I used these career talks as an opportunity to get some practice. I positioned myself as the "host" to introduce other guest speakers so had to get up on stage, talk about the festival, and then introduce the guest before then managing a Q&A session. I also had the opportunity to deliver some sessions with myself being the guest speaker based on my 20-year experience in the video games industry.

I pushed myself through the fear because my vision was stronger and bigger. I accepted that the experience would be uncomfortable, but I took the action anyway. I'm not saying that I suddenly became an amazing public speaker from this experience — far from it — but I am saying that now I feel a bit more comfortable being on stage and speaking to an audience.

Here's another mental image that I created. Skydiving. I was afraid of going skydiving because of what might happen — like the parachute not opening and me going splat on the ground. But I overcame this fear and did it anyway. One of my partner's friends was having a birthday and their brother was coming over to Dubai to celebrate for a week and together, they were planning to go skydiving. Because the opportunity was there, three of us — myself, my partner, and another friend — signed up to join them.

If you've never been skydiving when you do a tandem jump (two people together), you are paired with an instructor based on your size and weight. I was almost at the max weight limit allowed of 100kg, so the instructor I was paired with was really petite and slight of build which immediately sent my mind into overdrive. How on earth (pun intended!) was she going to manage to control me and the parachute and get us out of the plane and safely to the ground? We all went up in the same plane after having a briefing. I love the main skydive site in Dubai because it's close to Dubai Marina and the Palm with all the exotic hotels. You can sit in a pool or on a beach close by and watch the plane take off and then watch as all the skydivers gracefully descend back to earth.

As we got to the required altitude for jumping, I was starting to get really nervous. The flying part didn't bother me, my father was a pilot so I understood all about that bit and I know the ability to fly is in my blood. It was the jumping and the falling part that made me nervous.

The time came.

We shuffled to the exit door as those in the queue ahead of us had already made their leap of faith. I could hear the engines of the plane, and the wind rushing past and through the open door. There was a countdown and a little green light signalling it was time to go and I was suddenly thrust out into nothingness, tumbling head over heels in freefall. The wind streamed past my face and gave me that look you see in all the films when the skin is flapping in the wind.

And then suddenly, the instructor pulled the release on the parachute and my descent was halted. The canopy deployed, we slowed down and everything immediately became still and silent. There was literally no sound. As I looked around, I could see the iconic Dubai landmarks, the hotels on the Palm, and the outline of the fronds (these make up part of the design of the Palm), the Marina and the big towers, The Atlantis hotel, the Burj Al Arab off to one side.

I wrote that I'd watched skydivers from pools and beaches in Dubai and that they looked so graceful. Now in the midst of doing my own skydive, this is exactly what I felt. I was given control of the parachute through a handle I held in each hand and was able to turn left and right and take in the view.

It was serene and peaceful. It's a memory I will never forget. And I got to experience it because of breaking through the fear I had of what might happen — the mental image of going splat. That didn't happen and I had an amazing time.

Sadly, on the list of things I shouldn't do after my neck injury is skydiving because of the "snap" element when you stop freefall and the parachute opens and you very quickly slow down.

This mental image I had of going splat is the same sort of image we conjure up in other situations and that we let stop us. When we post something publicly to social media, we want the gratification of other people liking and commenting, but we also have this fear that whatever we post will be met with a negative reaction and so we stop ourselves from taking the action.

Mat Boggs, from the Brave Thinking Institute, told a story about this. He's a successful relationship/love coach and author but there was a time when he put off posting help videos on YouTube. It was something he'd always thought about but kept putting it off and kept putting it off until 5 years had passed. Finally, he took the plunge and started posting and now he has over 1M subscribers on YouTube and his videos have generated over 100M views. His regret is not starting to post his videos earlier and help more people.

In some instances, the action we are afraid of taking because of the possible response we might get is the very action we need to take to move us forward towards our vision.

The chapter on Chain #9 about Risk touched on this when I talked about my book and podcast. I had a fear that nobody would read, nobody would listen, and that I'd get laughed at or a negative response. The same was true when I set up the 4-day online training that I did for parents in June 2023.

But once we recognise what's causing the fear, and what impact it would have if the image we paint did come true, we start to gain power over it.

Depending on who and what you read, there is a line of thinking that the chemical reaction and sensation in your body that you get from fear/anxiety is actually the same as you get for nervous excitement. If we can channel that feeling in a positive way, sometimes the actions we need to take become a little easier.

We can also use visualisation techniques to help us work through the fear and imagine more positive scenarios. In Napoleon Hill's book "Think and Grow Rich", he talks about how thoughts become things. The more we think negatively, and fearfully, the more likely those negative scenarios become.

I've spoken to several people on the Unchained podcast about the topic of fear and Chloe King, who runs her own scuba diving centre, talked me through the process she takes students through who are new to scuba diving. First, it's about the equipment, becoming comfortable with it, what it does and how it feels when you wear it. The next step is to get into the pool and experience moving around in it. Then there's a process of practising with the regulator (the breathing bit you stick in your mouth) so you become familiar with breathing in and out through your mouth and into the mouthpiece of your regulator. Then there's the practice of taking it out of your mouth and putting it back in. All of these steps take place in the swimming pool well before getting onto a boat or walking into the water from the shore.

There's a structure and a set of steps Chloe takes people through to help them overcome their fear of the unknown when it comes to scuba. We also briefly talked about the fear of night dives. I had to do a night dive as part of my PADI Advanced Open Water qualification, and it was not a pleasant experience for me. My partner and I did it as a shore dive in Zanzibar, which meant the water was only 6m deep. I couldn't see very much so spent most of the time struggling with my buoyancy and bouncing between the surface and seabed. I also felt my torch wasn't penetrating the water enough. Like when you shine a torch against a wall and if you hold the torch really close to the wall, the beam spreads sideways a bit because it can't go through the wall. That's what I felt mine was like and so the whole experience proved stressful for me.

On the podcast, Chloe mentioned that some of her favourite dives have been night dives because she's able to see things she normally wouldn't. She can see the other divers in the group because they all have torches and it doesn't matter about the visibility being poor because you are focusing on things close to you, not in the distance. Hearing her talk about it in this way helped me change the mental image in my head to be one of a group of divers having fun waving their torches around and doing little dances with the beams of light, and seeing magical fish and sea creatures that I wouldn't see at any other time.

In another episode, one with Paul Raimon Massey, he talked me through his experience of being a boy soldier in the British Army, of signing up at the age of 16 to escape a challenging childhood and home situation, and the training he went through. Due to his age when he joined, there was an extended basic training for him and what he told me is that part of the training is about facing your fears head-on. There's white water rafting, abseiling and various other things to combat fears like drowning and heights. He got a sense that in any group of people, there will be some with a fear of heights, drowning, etc., and so everyone is put into these situations together so they can overcome that fear and recognise that they were actually strong enough physically and mentally to deal with those situations.

To give another example and short story about taking small steps to overcome fear, when my nephew turned 10, we went to the local climbing centre as he wanted to have the experience on the climbing walls. My niece and nephew were there, and I was there with my sister with us being the adults in the group.

I've had that mental image in my head of falling and so had always been reluctant to climb, even with a harness and cable. On this day, I decided to face it and wanted to get to the top of at least 1 climbing wall. I pushed myself through the worries and the sensations as I got higher and looked down towards the ground. As I got closer to the top, the adrenaline started pumping and I could feel my heart racing — I was way outside my comfort zone, but I'd taken the small steps that I needed to take, one handhold and foothold at a time. My nephew managed to get halfway up a few of the different climbing walls and my niece clipped in and gripped on but didn't actually start to climb. But that's completely okay because she took the first step, got clipped in, and got onto the wall. She took that first step. My nephew took a few more steps and had the opportunity to experience the feelings and sensations. In the future, he may push himself further and get to the top.

Okay, hopefully you now get my point. Fear is a mental image we create of what might happen and we have the ability to change that mental image. Sometimes, it changes because of something someone says. Other times, it is because we push through and have an experience that breaks the image we have and so we create a new, better image that isn't associated with fear.

## ACTIVITY #7 – Assessing Our Fears

*For this activity, I'd like you to write a list of all the things you fear about moving towards the items on your TALE Grid. This could be moving country and the mental image you create of it all going wrong. Or the mental image you create about changing jobs. Or the mental image of starting your own business and not getting any clients.*

*It doesn't matter what the fears are, or the mental images you've created as your worst case, this activity is about writing them down and recognising the "what ifs" that are flowing around in your head.*

*Once we have them on paper, we can start to address them when we look at the 4 steps to breaking the chains.*

# CHAIN #11 – Perception

Perception is another chain that holds us back and I view it in two different ways — the perceptions we have of people and situations, and the perceptions we have of what other people think of us and situations.

When it's dark outside and you look out the window and see a hooded figure, head bowed low, shuffling along the street, you might take the view that they are a little shady. This is a perception we create of the person and the situation. The reality could be very different; this person could be homeless and have a bad leg injury.

Everything in the world around us is viewed through the lens that we are wearing. We perceive things and then make judgements. What food looks good. What food looks bad. Which clothes in the shop window look good, and which patterns and colours look horrible together.

We also do the same with situations. What may be fun and exciting to one person might be a horrible experience for another person — like an escape room. Here's a funny, but also a horrible story, depending on your perception of the situation. My partner and I took her mum to an escape room experience in Dubai. The theme was Houdini, the great magician, illusionist, and escape artist. We had an hour to try and escape the room by solving some of the puzzles and overcoming the illusions. The starting activity in the room for the 3 of us was to be locked inside individual cages.

We were separated and each of us tried to work out how to get out of the cage we were placed in. I was in a stand-up cage with no lock on the bars or door. My partner was in a cage where the door looked like it had been fused shut and she was also placed in handcuffs and was sitting in a chair. Her mum was in a cage with a bench, a board on the wall, and a padlock on the cage door that required a key. So even if I was able to get free, or my partner was able to get free, we still couldn't get her mum out until we had found the key to unlock the padlock on her cage.

After a while of trying to escape the cages, we were given a hint of how I could get out of my cage which I did. Then it was all on me to help my partner and her mum escape. By this time, my partner had managed to find a way out of her handcuffs, so now it was about how to open the door that appeared welded shut, even though moments earlier she had walked into the cage.

I could tell at this point that mum was starting to get anxious of being locked in the cage. And in the conversations afterwards, she told us that she was worried that, she would be locked in there forever. This was her perception of the situation. For me and my partner, the perception was different. We perceived that if we couldn't get out of the cages, it was okay. After 60 minutes, we would have failed to escape and would have been let out of the cages by the game master who was monitoring everything through cameras in the ceiling.

This is an example of two very different perceptions of the same situation and demonstrates how our perception of a situation might not match up with the people around us, or society.

When I listened to a training session by Dean Graziosi and Matthew McConaughey in July 2023, they talked about journaling and Matthew looking back through his journals as he prepared to write his book 'Greenlights'. He made comments about the times he wrote down experiences of laughing at jokes and situations in the cinema that nobody else laughed at, or vice versa when everyone else laughed and he didn't. This was down to his perception of what was funny and what wasn't funny for his view of the world.

Our perception of people and situations is the first type of perception.

The second type of perception is the perception we create of what we think other people think.

Take a moment to read that again.

I know it sounds confusing so I'm going to try and break it down for you.

When we try and decide what to wear for a night out, sometimes we choose based on what we want to wear. Other times, we choose based on what we think the reaction will be from other people — their perception of us based on what we are wearing. We want them to have a good feeling or thoughts about us and so we choose to wear something we think they will like and, because of that, we think they will like us.

We are creating mental images. We are projecting and trying to imagine what other people will think and feel. The challenge with this is that it is a slippery slope and it can lead to being an eternal people pleaser rather than doing things for us, or because we want to.

Johanna Glavander explained this situation on the Unchained podcast. She worked in HR for several hotel chains until the pandemic hit and was laid off. Although initially dismayed at losing her job, she realised it was a time to focus on other priorities, like her two young children and wider family. Johanna also took some coaching qualifications and focused on people pleasing because it was something she recognised in herself.

During our chat, she mentioned that looking back, she realised that if she hadn't been as much of a people pleaser during her career, she would probably have progressed further.

But back to the point — worrying about other people's perceptions of us and being a people pleaser. The basic definition of being a people pleaser is continually saying yes to things, even when inside we don't want to. We worry about what the other person will say about it, or think about us, so we agree to go for the walk, attend the party, get involved in the project, look after someone else's kids, or stay out late.

The more we say yes to everyone else, the more we say no to ourselves.

I also want to make a quick side note — I'm not saying that you should say no to everything because there might be times when helping another person is just the right thing to do, like charity work, or helping a friend who is in a tough spot. It's a spectrum of choices and how often we say no. On one end of the spectrum where we don't say no, we become people pleasers, on the other end where we say no to everything, we become distant and unsociable. It's also important to highlight that when we say no, we aren't saying no to the person but we are saying no to the activity.

Johanna outlined that if we are constantly people pleasing and worrying about what people think of us, we lose out in at least 3 ways:

1) Our self-esteem and self-worth become linked to the actions we do for others as we seek praise and validation from them by saying "yes" to their requests, which means we feel uncomfortable standing separately or valuing ourselves for who we are as individuals

2) Our time disappears because we say "yes" to everyone else and not to ourselves, so we leave no room to work on the things, or do the things, that are important to us

3) Our internal melting pot can explode affecting those around us as the guilt and frustration buildup because we are not able to do what we want, or don't have the time to say yes to everything and worry that we will let someone down

She also referenced this as being like a downward spiral — we say yes so we lose time, we feel frustrated at not being able to do what we want, we have no time so we can't say yes to the next request, we feel frustrated and so the spiral goes downwards.

If you recognise yourself in what Johanna has outlined as her experience, then you might well fall into the category of being a people pleaser.

The same line of thought about saying yes to gain validation and worrying about what others think of us whether we say yes, or no, is also true about situations. We try to imagine what other people will think of our behaviour or in specific situations, and we let ourselves be led by those images we create in our head. We can't control what other people think or feel, however much we'd love to, because everyone is wired differently and as with the examples above — what may be funny for one person may not be funny for someone else.

I know I've been guilty of these things on more than one occasion. I've said or done things that haven't been entirely comfortable to me, but I've done them because of what I think another person is thinking of me.

There have also been times when I've flipped the script and not really cared about the perceptions of other people. Here's one example. I was asked to speak on a panel at a tech conference in Dubai. It was for start-ups and investors and the topic was about using gaming as a tool. There was a panellist from Google, one from a games company, who creates the games, and someone who helped brands use games for marketing campaigns. All 3 were dressed in black jeans/trousers and a dark-coloured t-shirt. The stage we were speaking on was outdoors in Dubai so the temperature was a little warm, even at 6 pm.

And what did I wear? Pink shorts and a flowery shirt. There are photos of the 4 of us sitting on the stage and me in the middle standing out from the rest because of the pink shorts. The moderator of the panel commented on my braveness. At a different event a few months later, he also commented to me that it inspired him to wear shorts and be more comfortable when attending events.

*At a tech conference in Dubai, in pink shorts and a flowery shirt*

I know my partner might not have fully forgiven me for another perceived clothing infraction — on one of our early "dates" when we went out for dinner with my parents, I chose to wear a pair of yellow trousers.

The same pair of yellow trousers also created a different set of perceptions several years later. In February 2023, I volunteered at the Dubai event that Mindvalley was hosting. If you aren't familiar with Mindvalley, it is a membership community with courses, events, and festivals around personal development, growth, spirituality, and a range of other topics. For the event in Dubai, I was assigned to help manage the VIP party in the evening and support VIP guests with getting into the party, crossing names off on a list, helping them understand the different activities that were on offer, which drinks were free and which were paid for separately, and any other information they needed.

I sat in the crowd for the whole day listening to the guest speakers for the event until it became time to prepare for the VIP party. I'd already decided that I was going to change my outfit for the evening and showcase some of my "personality". I had the yellow trousers in a bag ready to go because they were the brightest-coloured trousers I had at that time. I also had a bright blue jacket/blazer that I would normally wear for events and when I was guest speaking at conferences. I thought yes, a great combination of two bright colours to really show that colours are my thing. Can you see where this is going?

I went into the changing area and put on my yellow trousers, a nice flowery shirt and my bright blue jacket and then walked outside. Can you guess what happened next?

The first comment I received when I walked outside went something like this — "Oh, you are supporting Ukraine?"

Wow.

That wasn't the response I had expected at all. But the perception of this person was that the colours I was wearing were exactly the same as the Ukraine flag. And in reality, they were, but that wasn't the impression I was trying to create.

My perception was that these colours were bright and bold and would help me stand out. And they did, but for a very different reason. That one comment changed my whole perception of my clothes for the rest of the evening because I allowed it.

So, what's the point I'm trying to make here?

It's simply this.

We have the power to create our own perceptions and to change them. Other people will also create their own perceptions. The images that we create of what we think other people will think of us, or how we think other people will perceive us don't matter. If we continually worry about what other people will think, we will be scared to take action, or the action we take will be to please others.

If we can break this chain and worry less about what other people might think of us, we gain the ability to be free. Free to express ourselves and be who we truly are.

# CHAIN #12 — Pressure

Pressure. The feeling of something being squeezed or compressed until it bursts. I need to be aware of pressure when I'm scuba diving because the deeper I go, the greater the pressure is on my body.

And I think this is a nice starting point for us to talk about pressure. I split pressure into two camps.

The first is the pressure we put on ourselves. The scuba diving example above is something that falls into this first camp. I choose to go scuba diving and so I put myself into the position where pressure is acting on me. In the same way that I have always put pressure on myself to achieve, make progress, and win. I haven't always succeeded but I have a competitive spirit, and this is what helped me with the team sports I played and when I used to play video games in tournaments.

But we also put unnecessary pressure on ourselves. I spoke previously about the word "should" and how it is a dangerous word because it relates to expectations and can lead to feelings of guilt.

We drive ourselves to burnout trying to succeed. We work all the hours available. We get frustrated if something doesn't happen fast enough. We put pressure on ourselves to make changes and make a difference.

Burnout was another topic on the podcast episode where I spoke to Freddie Pullen. He talked about his experience of working with entrepreneurs and how minor aesthetic changes to the environment, like more green plants, can reduce stress levels and feelings of pressure.

Internally, we are our own worst critics. Inside my head, there's regularly been a voice grabbing me by the scruff of the neck and shaking me while asking questions around why I haven't done something, or why I'm afraid, or why I freeze when I know the action I need to take.

Okay. I've painted enough of a picture here. Once we recognise that we put pressure on ourselves, we can begin to give ourselves a bit of grace and the time and space necessary to continue working towards our goals and vision, even if they take a little longer.

With my new acceptance that the universe has a plan, when I start to beat myself up, I take a step back and look at the bigger picture. As long as I'm making progress and taking action, then I'll give myself a break because some things need time to compound. Other things may be waiting for the right person or right conversation to happen. The negative self-talk inside our heads can have a negative impact on our actions and our bodies. The reverse is true — I healed a broken neck with positive internal talk.

So, what's the second camp when it comes to pressure?

The second camp is the pressure we let ourselves feel from other people. The stares and the looks. The requests to do things. The attempted manipulation to have you conform to society in a certain way like the way you dress, what you say, and how you behave.

We can feel this pressure. It seeps into us like a mouldy green fog if we let it. Over time, it corrodes us from the inside. We feel like there is a 1 million-ton weight on our shoulders and eventually, we snap, break or go pop.

You and I may have fallen victim to the same sort of societal pressures — go to college or university to get a piece of paper and then get a job so we can pay taxes, and then ultimately feel like we are living in a hamster wheel with the same things day in and day out. I certainly did the university one — and I did it twice so that I could get a Master's degree but I also started to break the system from that early point. I set up my first business as soon as I finished university and was able to secure client projects for companies like Microsoft and Telefonica. The 2008/09 financial crisis led me to closing that business and spending a month on holiday through the summer and then it led me to the opportunity at EA SPORTS to work on FIFA, but that's another example of where I didn't fully give in to the external pressure.

As I was preparing to close the business down, I started having interviews for jobs and successfully got a role as a winter rep for Crystal Ski. There were still a few months to go until that started, but it meant I had something for the winter period and beyond. I would be in a different country supporting people on their vacations, I would be earning, and my accommodation and flights would be covered.

With time to wait until that role started, I went and spent a month in the party capital of Cyprus visiting a few friends who were out there working the summer season and having a blast. Each day of the month was pretty much a rinse and repeat — sleep in, get up and grab some food, have a bit of time in the sun and then come back, get ready to go out partying, sit in a bar drinking until my friends finished their shifts and then we would all carry on until the early hours, sometimes even going long enough to see the sunrise.

I had my laptop with me so was checking emails and still applying for other jobs. While I was in Cyprus, I got offered an interview with EA SPORTS. It was for FIFA, a game I hadn't really played very much since the World Cup 1998 version on my PC, and in a role I hadn't done before. It was also a contract role compared with the Crystal Ski role which was a permanent position.

The EA SPORTS role would mean moving to Guildford and being in the office, paying for accommodation, and having less stability because of the contract status (I would actually be contracted to a 3rd party who would pay me after getting timesheets and approvals from EA SPORTS that I had done the work).

After the interview, when I got offered the job, I had a decision to make. The external pressure was to go for the stability of the Crystal Ski role and all the perks it provided, but I knew for me it wasn't the right move. EA SPORTS presented an opportunity to stay involved in the games industry, learn something new and gain some valuable experience. Don't get me wrong, working as a rep would have also given me some valuable experience and I have a friend who did exactly that role for many years and loved it. But I knew it wasn't right for me based on the two opportunities I had on the table.

I didn't give in to the external pressure. And if I didn't give in, it means you don't have to either. Sure, there will be times when it is the path of least resistance and you can stomach it because it's a necessary evil and a stepping stone, but at least you make that conscious decision. The danger is when we blindly bow to the pressure of others.

In history, this would be called oppression. This is what we need to break free of and break this chain. We need to regain the power and the ability to recognise the external pressure from society, friends, family, and work, and then make an informed decision. A decision that sits well with us. A decision that won't leave us feeling bitter towards the world around us.

You have that power inside you. In the next part of this book, I want to help you unlock it and unleash it so that you can become unchained.

Over the past 12 chapters, we've looked at the 12 invisible chains that hold us back in life, make us feel stuck and frustrated, and prevent us from living the life we dream of, and achieving the goals and vision we have.

Now, we head to the point of regaining our power and learning the 4-step process for breaking each of the chains so that we can move forward and make progress.

# Part 3
# Break The Chains and Finally Find Freedom

In Part 2, we uncovered the 12 invisible chains that hold us back in life. Now in Part 3, it is time to explore the steps we can take to start breaking them.

The first thing we will do is look at the 3 different types of chains and how they fit together, including which ones are the easiest to break first. This will give you a guide and a plan on which ones to try and tackle first in your own life so that you can see, feel, and experience some quick wins.

Then we will look at the 4 steps to breaking the chains and the process you can repeat at any time to help you move forward towards the vision, goals, and desires you created in your TALE Grid in Part 1 of this book.

Finally, in the last few chapters, we look at how to reinforce what you've learned, take action, and finally find the freedom you've been longing for.

I know you have the power to do this. We all have the power to do this. The question is whether we let ourselves use that power.

And to help you use your power, if you haven't already, you can download the free supporting pack of materials and resources at www.finallyfindfreedom.com/resources.

Anyway, let's now focus on Part 3 and the 3 different types or levels of chains and how we can break these chains that hold us back. I've used "types" and "levels" interchangeably because there are 3 different types, which you will read about in the next chapters. But each of these types can also be stacked, like levels, because one type of chain is easier to break than another.

If you break one type of chain, it becomes easier to move on to breaking the next type of chain and then on to the 3rd type of chain until you've almost moved up in levels. Your ability to break the chains will have improved and so you begin to focus on the hardest chains to break.

# Understanding The 3 Types of Chains

When I first created this model, I had written down the 12 different chains as they related to my life, the things I was trying to work through, and the things I had already managed to break through in little pieces.

There had been some successes — like breaking through the fear and knowledge chains to write and publish my first book — but there were also some big and scary chains.

The more I looked at the chains to try and simplify things in my head so that I could work towards taking action, I realised there were some similarities between the chains. This helped me group them together into 3 levels or types of chains.

It also helped me re-order the chains so that as I was looking through them and talking to other people about them, it became easier to describe them and the process for breaking them.

Knowledge, Speed, Convenience, and Relationships were focused on the things we can control and the actions we can take. Whether we give into convenience and take a different action, how we perceive the speed of change and progress, how we fill the knowledge gap, and which relationships we choose to keep or move away from. These were all action-based chains and so the first type of chain is exactly that — the self-directed actions.

From this starting point, I then looked at the remaining 8 chains. Time, Location, Priorities, and Responsibilities stood out as things that are often influenced by others. Our location may be influenced by our job or family, our priorities influenced by other people's priorities, or our responsibilities given to us by other people, and even how we use our time is often influenced by other people. This second type or level of chain became about external influences and how other people have an impact on us.

Then it was about the final 4 chains of Risk, Fear, Perception, and Pressure. It could be argued that some of these could fit into the external influence level or type of chain, but I got a sense that these 4 actually fit together. You may already have an idea of what this type of chain is based on how I've written some of the chapters. It is about the mental images that we create.

The mental images we create about situations that might happen, the images in our head of what we think other people think about us, the pictures we paint about what we believe society is telling us to do.

Here's an example from my own life of the mental images. I have a distrust of large dogs. Growing up, I had small dogs in the family — a cocker spaniel called Chloe with her big floppy ears swinging left and right as she ran around the garden.

One day my best friend and I, the one who lived 4 doors away and that I'd grown up with, went over to the house of another friend close to where we lived. I was probably about 12 or 13 years old. In the house, there was a much larger dog than I was used to — I think it was a Labrador or something like that. We'd been round to this friend's house many times before with no drama. But on this particular day, something sparked the dog into action. As my best friend went to stroke this dog, it sunk its teeth into the palm of his hand.

He later needed several stitches. This one experience has coloured my perception of large dogs since then. It's silly because I know smaller dogs can do exactly the same thing, and it wasn't an experience that directly happened to me as I wasn't the one who got bitten. But I now have a mental image of a past experience that has shaped my thinking. This is the power of mental images and why these 4 chains of Risk, Fear, Perception, and Pressure are all about the mental images we create in our minds and why they are the hardest chains to break.

So here are the 3 types of chains in order:

- **Self-Directed Actions (Knowledge, Speed, Convenience, Relationships)**
- **External Influences (Time, Location, Priorities, Responsibilities)**
- **Mental Images (Risk, Fear, Perception, Pressure)**

Now that we know there are 3 types of chains to break through, we can begin to decide which ones to break first and understand which ones are the easiest to focus on.

The self-directed actions are the best starting point because those are things we can immediately control and make changes around.

We can decide to spend less time watching TV.

We can decide and take action to fill a knowledge gap that we've identified.

We can decide which relationships are draining us and take action to move away from them.

We can become more comfortable with the different speeds that we and the world operate at.

There is a power inside of us if we choose to use it. And once we start to take action and make changes, it becomes easier to make more changes.

I decided to give up alcohol because it was a convenience, and I was tired of feeling like rubbish for 2 days after a brunch in Dubai.

I've been on a personal development journey since 2021 to fill the knowledge gap and gain new understanding, skills, and ways of operating.

I've distanced myself from business relationships that were draining me.

If I've been able to decide to make changes and do these things, then you too have the power to make changes in your life. Your changes may be completely different from mine but that's okay — we are all different people. What I'm trying to highlight here is that we all have this power if we choose to use it.

Once we start to make progress breaking through these 4 chains of Knowledge, Speed, Convenience, and Relationships at level 1, the chains focused on self-directed actions, it becomes easier to work on the other chains. Changing your actions around areas of convenience can free up time for you to work on other things, or to fill the knowledge gap. Filling the knowledge gap may enable you to break through the chain related to location at level 2 or change your responsibilities and so on.

There are links and connections between each of the chains so breaking through 1 will have an impact on all the others.

Some of the fears I've been able to break through are because I broke through the knowledge chain first. In the same way, some of the perceptions I had about things, and what I thought others would think of me, were easier to overcome because I broke the knowledge chain and did away with conveniences.

Now we have an understanding of how the chains fit together and the 3 different types, it is time to look at the 4 steps to breaking them. In the next chapter, I'll describe each step so that you have a repeatable process you can use to break through and break free in your own life.

# The 4 Steps to Breaking a Chain

Chains are known for being tough. They are meant to hold and to bind. And that's one of the reasons I chose them as a reference point, because of the imagery they create in a lot of people's minds.

But like anything, there are ways to break through them; in the real world, it might be with a pair of bolt-cutters, or extreme heat to melt the whole chain. For the purposes of this book, I'm not suggesting anything so drastic or dangerous, but I do want to provide you with something that's helped me because having steps to follow is something that makes sense in my head. I'll admit I don't always follow all the steps and sometimes read ahead to see what's next before I complete the step before, but I feel more comfortable knowing there are steps to follow.

Anyway, let us get down to it.

Throughout the chapters focusing on each of the chains, I often wrote about assessing things. This is the first step we can take in breaking through a chain.

### Step 1 – Assess

When starting on a journey, it helps to know where we are starting from. Even if we plug in a destination to a satnav, it will still determine a route based on our starting position whether we input our starting position or not.

We can do the same for each of the chains.

Before I go and do the weekly food shopping, I'll look through the cupboards to see what we've used up, or running out of, and that helps me create my list. We can take an inventory of our current lives in the same way.

The best starting point for this is by looking at it through the lens of the first 4 chains — the ones related to self-directed action. If we take an inventory of the actions we take, like the activities and how we spend our time, we can identify which activities are helping us break the knowledge chain and which are strengthening the convenience chain. This is why I set you the activity of recording all your activities and the amount of time you spend on each of them so we can use that list in this first step — we can assess our current reality.

I try and read on a regular basis, and I've already mentioned I watch webinars and trainings to help me break the knowledge chain. That's what helped me write and publish my first book and launch my podcast. I used some of my time to gain the knowledge I needed.

We can also take an inventory of our relationships at both a personal level and a professional, business level. If we rate them on the scale of positive to negative, we can see any relationships we feel icky about or that score 6 or lower. These are the ones we should focus on removing ourselves from, or dramatically reduce the amount of time and effort we spend on, because if they are marked that low, it's clear they are relationships that drain which is not beneficial to our long -term goals and vision.

I know this sounds brutal but the path to freedom isn't always easy. The situation we are in right now is because of the decisions and situations in our past. To break free of them and move forward, we may have to make some tough decisions with our future in mind.

The next part of assessing our current reality is a more positive spin on things — we can create a list of the things we enjoy doing and want to spend more time on or want to learn. Effectively, we will have a list of "do more of/see more of" and a list of "do less of/see less of". It's a visual representation of things that might have been swimming around in our heads.

When I watched an online training session with Dean Graziosi and Matthew McConaughey, they talked about journaling and how Matthew had been journaling for over 30 years. When he wrote his book Greenlights, he looked back through his journals and was able to identify patterns.

Some of these patterns of behaviour enabled him to make massive progress while other patterns sent him backwards.

Using our "do more of" and "do less of" lists mean we can clearly see in black and white the negative patterns that will keep us stuck and the things that will fuel us and make us start to feel better about life.

This step of assessing our current life and situation is also something we can and should repeat on a regular basis. It can help us to focus on the next actions we need to take to feel more free in our current reality.

In his book "The Code of the Extraordinary Mind", Vishen talks about Blissipline and having a vision for the future but also living in the now and being grateful for it. It becomes easier to live in the now and be grateful if there are fewer things that are dragging us down. He also talks about the power of gratitude and how it is now scientifically proven that gratitude can give us more energy, help us develop a more forgiving attitude, be less depressed and less anxious, feel more socially connected, help us get better sleep, and have fewer headaches.

In the training session with McConaughey, he also talked about being intentional. Matthew gave the example of mixing sundowner drinks because "it was 5 o'clock somewhere in the world" until he took a step back and asked himself the question of whether he was doing it out of habit and the general flow of what he'd always done, or whether he was being intentional and actually wanted the drink.

If you've been doing the highlighted activities throughout the previous chapters in this book, you will already have assessed key areas of your life against some of the 12 chains. If you haven't done those activities yet, now is your opportunity to do them before moving on. And to make it a little easier, there's a section at the back of the book where all the activities are listed out, in order, so you can work through them.

I also just wrote about the "do more/do less" list. This is something you can also create now before we move on to Step 2 of breaking the chains.

## ACTIVITY #8 – Create a Do More/Do Less List

*On a piece of paper, create two columns. At the top of one column, write "Do More Of" and at the top of the other write "Do Less Of".*

*Now, under each heading, write a list of the activities that you want to do more and do less of.*

*These lists can be anything you like, some taken from your TALE Grid, others may come from your 7-day Activity Log.*

### Step 2 – Understand

Once we have assessed our current reality, got our lists of do more/ do less, thought about the relationships that drain us, and when/if we are supporting ourselves in gaining new knowledge, we can start beginning to understand.

When I say "understand" what I'm actually talking about is understanding our current patterns, our next steps, the practices and techniques that might help us make changes, and the shifts in our thinking.

Once we understand all of these, we can move onto the third step. Before we go there, I just want to expand on what I mean by "understanding the practices and techniques that might help us make changes".

It's important for us to know what does and doesn't work, what has and hasn't worked for others, the perceived difficulty of doing something, or how long it is going to take. In this book, I'm sharing what's worked for me, but there are all sorts of books about morning routines, gratitude practices, sleep routines, creating habits and more. I've read a good number of them.

So, I'd like to share my perspective on these things so that you can make your own judgement, understand your options, and then decide which things to try, or not try, before you move to step 3.

First, let's talk about gratitude and meditation. It's something I've grown to do more of over the years because I've recognised the calming effect it has on me. Some people like to do it in the morning, some just before bed, others do it multiple times a day. And there are lots of different ways of doing gratitude practices and meditation.

I have a really busy mind with thoughts and ideas bouncing around all the time so just having peaceful music doesn't work for me. I prefer to have guided meditation so there's a voice I can focus on and instructions about what to visualise. The 6-phase meditation by Vishen Lakhiani is one I do quite regularly because it has phases focused on gratitude, vision, and forgiveness. Research suggests that forgiveness practices can give a major boost to your overall wellbeing as it enables you to become more at peace with everything that's happened in your past, and be more open to situations that happen in the now and in the future.

I try to do at least 5-10 minutes a day where I also spend time thinking about my future, what I'd like to achieve and how I want to live — the freedom I'm looking for in my life.

In the introduction to this book, I talked about making the decision to spend more time outdoors and introducing the practice of walking to the golf club to be out in nature. I try and spend some time outdoors like this a few times a week. I don't have a morning routine that's set in stone, but there are a few things that I try to weave in, like this outdoor time. I'm a big list person and a fan of "to do" lists, so if I haven't created one the night before and set my intentions then I'll create my list of priorities for the day. It helps me stay mindful of the tasks I need to complete that will move me forward and also enables me to prioritise my time.

Which leads nicely to the use of time. Time boxing and habit stacking are two practices I use in this area. Time boxing is about setting dedicated time in the calendar for activities and committing to them. It could be having a coaching call at the same time every week, a daily commitment and time allocated to the gym or working out, time focused on creating content or a million other activities but the point is, if it's in the calendar it's something I'm more likely to do.

I also habit stack which is the practice outlined by James Clear in his book Atomic Habits. It's when you introduce new activities immediately on the back of something that you already do so that over time it becomes a new habit. A silly example could be doing 5 pushups every time you go to get a drink of water. The original action was to go and get a drink of water to keep hydrated and the pushups are what's being stacked on top.

I've given an overview of some of the things I do as part of my life, but the key to this second step about understanding is for you to take the time to think about what makes sense for you and your life. You might be more spiritual than me, or you might not, you might live in a completely different location or climate, or you might have a different family situation. That's why I'm not prescribing a one-size-fits-all approach — it's about the process.

Gaining an understanding of the options available to us, whether that's meditation, timeboxing, morning routines, walking in nature or anything else, enables us to make a decision about what to try which leads us to step 3 in the process of breaking the chains — Introduce.

### Step 3 – Introduce

To make changes in our life and move forward, we need to become the person that we see in our visions. That person isn't the person we are right now, and I recognised that in myself. For the visions I had, I knew I needed to become more comfortable with public speaking and so when the opportunity came up to do career talks in schools, I grabbed it. Over a 3-week period, I did 10 sessions, some of them as a host and some of them as a guest speaker. I'm still a work in progress when it comes to public speaking but this early opportunity enabled me to get more practice and become more comfortable.

I introduced myself to this situation so that I could gain the practice and move forward. There may be situations like this that come up in your life where you can gain the practice you know you need to help you become the person you see in your visions, who has achieved what you want and is living the life you dream of.

The other type of introduction is where we introduce things into our life rather than introduce ourselves into new situations. What activities can we introduce, or behaviours, that will move us forward? What can we swap in and out that will break the convenience chain, or any of the other chains that we want to break?

Maybe you try and get together for a coffee morning with all the people that fuel you so that once a week, you see these people and feel good. Perhaps it's the chains of fear and risk that you want to break, so introducing a meditation routine may be a solution to help quieten your mind and help you focus on more positive aspects of life.

In the previous step about understanding, I talked about time boxing, habit stacking, gratitude practices, and meditation as some of the things that I've introduced to help me. This Introduce step is about helping you start to introduce and test new things in your own life.

I'm not here to tell you exactly what to introduce because we are all different with different views of the world. What I am here to do is suggest that introducing new activities, mindset practices, and behaviours can enable you to move forward towards your dreams and life of freedom.

And sometimes to introduce something new, we need to drop something old. That's one of the reasons I talked about the "do less of" list and the list of people and relationships that drain you so it becomes easier for you to say no. Saying no, or doing less of the negative list, can free up time and energy that you can use to introduce and test these new activities and practices.

Dropping the extra episode on Netflix could see you introduce more reading to fill the knowledge gap, or use that time for meditation and gratitude practices.

Identifying the activities or habits you already have will enable you to see opportunities to introduce new things straight after, so you begin habit stacking. If, like me, you like writing lots of lists of "to do" items, perhaps transferring them into time boxes on your calendar will provide more structure and a way to work through your list.

This is the essence of the Introduce step — starting to test new practices, behaviours, and ways of thinking to see which help us move forward while also breaking the chains.

### Step 4 – Repeat

The final step is about repeating what works. And when I say "what works" I'm talking about giving something a period of time to become embedded in your life. New habits can take up to 60 days to become embedded so if you only give something 3 days, it is unlikely to cause a significant change in your life. This is even more true if you then stop doing it and revert back to what you were doing before.

So my guidance here is to be mindful that some things will take time to become a normal part of your life. And then if, after a reasonable amount of a test run, you decide it's not something for you, try something new.

It took me a while to find the things that work for me. And one of the best things I found was not something I found in a book. Over the years, I've gotten to a point where I know I'm most creative when it comes to ideas, creating strategy, and problem solving when I sit in a coffee shop with blank A4 pages and my headphones on and listening to music. Normally, it's house music or electronic dance music because that's what I grew up listening to. This is my "coffee and cake" time and it's where I've created some of the frameworks in this book, course outlines, the outlines for books, solutions to client projects, the responses to RFPs, and client briefs and so much more.

This is something that I've found works for me and is now a part of the way I operate. I know if I have something I need to do some creative thinking about, then being in the office or a place where I spend most of my time is not the best space for me. I've also habit stacked this activity — when I do a walk to the golf club to spend more time outside, before I do the walk back, I spend some time making notes while having a coffee and listening to music. And when I do the walk itself, I'll listen to a podcast so I'm exercising both my mind and my body. If I'm in the UK, then I'll walk to a coffee shop and make notes. Sometimes, the catalyst is because I have something I need to think about and work through so the walk is a nice by-product. Other times, I need to get out and have a walk so I take the opportunity to sit and think.

The same is true for new business activities. If you are an entrepreneur, or want to set up your own business, there will be things that need repeating regularly in order for you to make progress. Whether that's outreach to potential customers, creating content on a regular basis, speaking at events, or sending emails out, it doesn't matter; there will be things that you will need to do for your specific business that are things you will need to repeat.

Which means the key is to think about how you can introduce them into your daily life and then turn them into repeated actions or habits.

And this is a great point to introduce the concept of structures. It's something I first came across during a podcast conversation with Don Armand. Don is a former international rugby player for England, Premiership and European champion, so he's had a period as a professional sportsman. Now he's retired from playing and moved into business coaching.

During our conversation, he noted that we are all high-performance athletes underneath, but the thing that makes professional athletes different is the structures. There is a structure for training, for nutrition, for recovery, and for match day. There are things the professional athletes do in each of those situations, the steps they take or the processes they follow.

Having and knowing these structures enables them to move on autopilot for certain parts of the day, which means they can conserve energy and focus on other things.

It's likely we already have some structures in our day, like how we brush our teeth, how we make a cup of coffee in the morning, or how we make our bed. Don's point is that if we introduce more structures to our lives, we create repeatable actions that will help us move forward. Write a weekly email at the same time every week, record and post a video at the same time every day and, in the same way, have a regular release schedule for a new podcast episode or the process for recording the podcast episode. These are all structures that I created to help make my life easier so that I knew what I was doing and had something repeatable.

These 4 steps of Assess, Understand, Introduce, and Repeat are steps that you can use throughout your life in many different areas. And if you were expecting some magic pill, shooting star, or bag of stardust, I'm sorry. You may have read this section and said to yourself that there's nothing new here and, to be honest, you are absolutely right. I've not re-invented the wheel but hopefully, I've provided a different perspective and frame of reference for you to view things from and to help you actually make changes and become the person you need to be so that you can achieve the vision you have for your life.

Now, it is about time for us to finally find freedom and that's what I want to talk about in the final chapters of this book.

## Protecting Yourself With the Word No

No is a difficult word for a lot of us to say. We feel the need to say yes for a number of reasons like reducing potential conflict, getting someone to like us, or taking the easier option when presented with a choice.

But if we continue saying yes, we'll say yes to the extra slice of cake, extra episode, taking on extra work from the boss, agreeing to each and every thing that comes our way.

To achieve freedom in our lives, we need to feel comfortable saying no. When I made the decision to give up alcohol, I was making a commitment to constantly say no to every offer of a drink or a shot.

Saying no is actually a way of protecting ourselves, and it does this in two ways. The first is the protection of our time. We've already talked about time being a chain and how we abuse our time in combination with convenience to stay stuck. If we want to break free, we need to make better use of our time and say no to the convenient things in our life, like the extra episode of Netflix, or playing video games for hours and hours (yes, I've been very guilty of this over the years).

The second way that saying no protects us is about our wellbeing. If we say yes, we increase the risk of putting ourselves in positions, or undertaking activities, that we don't want to be in or don't want to do.

This is what I outlined in the chapter about the perception chain and the discussion about people pleasing I had with Johanna.

You may be reading all of this thinking it's hard to say no to some things in case you hurt people's feelings but in reality, they will respect your honesty. It's better to say no and cause a momentary unrest than to say yes and feel like you are losing a bit more of your soul and that you are dying inside, with a fake smile on your face, as you do another activity that you really don't want to do.

When you learn to say no, it means you can say yes to the things that are important to you, the things that truly matter, and the things that mean something to you. You can keep yourself positively charged and then give all your energy and focus to the things you do say yes to.

The alternative is saying yes to the things you don't want to do, having your energy drained and not showing up as your true authentic self. I know which situation I'd rather be in. There are many things I've said no to over the years including holidays, other people's birthdays, celebratory drinks, days out, taking on extra work or a project, enquiries from companies wanting a service I don't provide and many more.

When you say no to something, you also don't need to think of a justification like the dog ate your homework, you left the washing in, or you are having your hair done. A simple "I can't, I already have plans" is all it takes. You don't need to expand on what those plans are or justify yourself to anyone but, for the purposes of this book, the plans you have are the commitments you've made to yourself to progress towards your goals and dreams and the freedom you want in your life. I mentioned in the chapter about perception that when you say no, you are saying no to the activity and not to the person. This is an important distinction to make.

Getting sucked into situations you don't want to be in and that have the potential to cause a negative charge in you are things that are unlikely to help you make progress.

It does take a bit of practice to become comfortable saying no but after a while, it begins to feel natural.

I also want to make a point about indecision or going with the flow. This is the equivalent of saying yes to someone else or an activity. You have not given a definitive no and, if you are going with the flow, you are taking the path of least resistance which is not a vote in favour of progressing towards freedom.

Jack Canfield, in 'How to get from where you are to where you want to be', sums this up nicely with the statement:

> ***"It is time to stop looking outside yourself for the answers to why you haven't created the life and results you want, for it is you who creates the quality of the life you lead and the results you produce."***

He also goes on to talk about us taking 100% responsibility for everything in our lives, the good and the bad, and that we are never really stuck. We are just stuck in a repeating pattern where we re-create the same experience over and over because we haven't changed our thinking, beliefs, behaviour, or the words we say.

Continually saying yes to everyone else keeps us stuck in the repeating pattern, and it isn't until we start to change our behaviour, and what we say, that the pattern will break and we will start to experience changes.

If all of this makes you feel a little uncomfortable, let us start with the small things, and a double whammy of breaking some of the chains.

Start by saying no to the conveniences. These are little things like the extra slice of pizza, ordering a takeaway (takeout), or an extra episode. You can think of what you are doing like building a muscle. It takes repetition of a workout to build muscle. Starting to say no to the small things will help you feel like you are making progress, and it will also build the muscle so you become more comfortable saying no to the bigger things and the "asks" that get put in front of you.

Once you've mastered the power of saying no, and you've demonstrated to yourself that the world doesn't end when you do say no, you also gain the freedom to start making bigger changes in your life.

# Breaking Free of the 9-5

I've already mentioned in earlier parts of this book the research I did when I was writing the first draft and that a lot of the responses were from people who wanted more time, especially more time with family.

Now, in order to have more time, there needs to be some thought given as to how we can generate money so that we don't have to work all the hours available and can actually make good on that desire for more family time.

On my entrepreneurial journey since the age of 16, I've had many ups and downs, some wins, and some losses. From that journey, and the evolution of my own life, I'd like to give a few thoughts if you are aiming to break free of the 9-5.

Firstly, give some thought on what skills and experiences you have. We aren't looking to trade time for money if we can help it because that's exactly what we do in a traditional job. Our boss pays us based on the number of hours we work and the value we bring to their business.

If you have skills and experience, you may be able to turn that into courses, coaching, workshops, or retained services for other people. That's certainly the approach that I took when I redesigned my business in the middle of 2023. I reached a point where I knew doing ad-hoc projects wasn't going to get me to where I wanted to be. I was sometimes time-rich when I was between projects, but I had the hit-and-miss element on finances. Waiting for invoices to be paid, negotiations around contracts, having to pay suppliers and sometimes being left with very little due to the client's budget.

My suggestion is to avoid creating something that's project-based unless you can find people to do business development for you so that you can roll from one project to another without any gaps. But even then, if you can do that, there's a question of whether that eats more time or less time. From my experience, projects can be a time suck with change requests from clients, waiting for approvals, meetings about meetings and so on. I don't know about you but this doesn't sound like freedom to me.

Dean Graziosi and Tony Robbins are big supporters of teaching what you know and the experiences you've had, even the painful ones, because you might just be able to help someone else avoid the pain you went through. I'm not saying everyone should do that, but it's certainly one route.

Another route I've come across in the past is more aligned with freelancing and the "workstyle" movement pioneered by Alex Hirst and Lizzie Penny at Hoxby. They built a network of professionals from all walks like marketing, PR, tech, social media, accounting and legal. When projects came in members of the network could pitch their services and support, and suggested number of hours based on their availability, creating a project team specifically for that project or client.

One key consideration with all of this comes down to how much money you think you need to live the life that you've dreamed of and written in your TALE Grid. If you have a figure in mind, then you can reverse engineer that to help you think about how you can generate the required level of income.

Some of the work I do with people looking to break free of the 9-5, and entrepreneurs, is about working out how they can do more with less time, and set themselves up to generate money without spending lots of time.

This might sound crazy, but one of the key principles is about focused effort and repetition and why things like courses, workshops, and coaching is a fast-growing industry. Those approaches mean you can design the business to suit your lifestyle while also supporting hundreds and thousands of people if that's what you want.

The important part is to work out what makes the most sense for you and where you are trying to get to. Finding the balance between work and time spent is a key consideration for freedom. You might be sitting there asking, why should you work at all? It's a great question so here's my answer.

Without meaningful work, we get bored. We need to have something to focus our attention on and something we feel we are making a contribution to which supports others. If you spend every day golfing, lunching with the ladies, or relaxing on the beach, it will get very repetitive and dull after a while.

There needs to be that balance of work and time on other things. It's one reason why in the chapter about the TALE Grid, I asked how much time you want to spend each day working.

Which takes us back to the question of what work to do.

Some of the responses to the market research were from people aiming to grow their business and sell it. While that's a noble endeavour, it's also not without risks. You need to grow to a size that's interesting for someone else to acquire you, you need to find someone you are willing to sell to, you need to agree on figures and terms, and you need to agree on what the "after" looks like for you and the company. It can be tough to let go of something you've built, and I know that from experience when I finally made the decision to close down previous businesses that I had.

I've tried to compile a few of the different routes and approaches into a table so that you can see the differences between them when it comes to time and money, but this is just based on my view of the world and my experiences. I'm not putting my hand up and telling you these are the only ways to do it, or that in each route, there's a specific way of building an income stream as is proven by the stories I shared of Dino and Eddy, who generate money from selling courses about growing an audience on Twitter/X and that's all they focus on. It's coaching and courses but in a very specific area.

Here's the table.

| ROUTE | TIME | MONEY | LEVERAGE |
|---|---|---|---|
| | | | |
| Courses, Coaching, Masterminds, and Workshops | Can be designed in a way where you keep control of your time while still being able to support and serve people. | Unlimited potential as a course, can be eternally available and you can have hundreds or thousands of people on virtual workshops or in a coaching program. | Med-High |
| Freelancing | You can manage your time freedom based on the work that you accept but you may also need to spend time finding the work. | Income is often more limited as it's dependent on the services you provide and tied to the amount of time you're available. | Low-Med |
| Project-Based Business | Very similar to a freelancer with more time freedom when you aren't working on a project but, like a freelancer, you might need to spend time finding the next project | Fees for projects can vary depending on the duration and scope of work. This provides flexibility to earn more for different types of projects. | Low-Med |

| | | | |
|---|---|---|---|
| Service-Based Business | If you can build your business in a way that provides a retained service, you can manage your time and bring in other people to support you. | Limited by the number of clients you can serve but the retainer fees can help you towards freedom. | Med-High |
| Growth Partner | Able to choose how much time you give to your clients in a similar way to freelancing or a service-based business. | The big difference between being a growth partner and a service-based business is the potential financial upside. You negotiate a percentage of revenue based on what you help a client achieve. | High |

At the end of the table, I've briefly touched on working as a Growth Partner and this is something I want to quickly expand on a little bit because it was something new to me. The others I was already familiar with and had dabbled in. Service-based businesses with retainers have been around for years and you can build those types of businesses around anything from being a gardener on retainer to someone who writes and posts on social media accounts for other people.

Being a Growth Partner means you are directly invested in the success of your client and the results you can get for them. You may have agreed on a small retainer so that you have something on the books, but the bulk of any upside comes from what you deliver. If you agree you'll get paid 10% of everything you generate for the client and you help them add another $1 Million to the business, that would be $100,000 for you. If you have the knowledge and experience, a minor change in the business that takes you 4 hours to talk people through and implement could net you that extra $100,000 (the 10%).

This is something I've seen in some of the online spaces I've frequented with Growth Partners helping course creators and coaches increase the size of their business in exchange for a piece of the revenue. Sometimes, these people are selective with their clients so there's a greater chance to get that 10% or 20%, but it's a different model in the world of online business.

## The Power of Leverage

Leverage is something I've been aware of for a number of years, but it wasn't until I heard Alex Hormozi talk about it multiple times that it really clicked for me in the context of finding freedom.

If we continually trade time for money, it becomes harder to break free of the rat race and the 9-5, unless the output we generate is so disproportionate to the input. What I mean by this is that if you are a freelancer trading time for money, and the service you provide is graphic design and you charge based on the time, or the number of images you create, then you might be doing something you enjoy doing (creativity and variety), but your freedom will be restricted. It will be restricted because you can only create so many images, have so much time to create those images, and need to adhere to the brief from the client. This is the type of work that sits on one end of the scale.

At the other end of the scale is the Growth Partner who can generate more output for the input. They put in 1 hour of work, and because they have a skill or specialist knowledge, they can generate direct income or value for a client. They can walk away with $100,000 like in the example I used previously.

The project-based businesses and service-based businesses often sit in the middle. They can optimise processes to help increase the output for each input, which is normally time or money. A project-based business can only serve the number of clients or projects based on the number of project teams it builds. This was the model I had for many years which I now look back on and hold my hand up and say it was something that held me back.

Another way of looking at leverage is about creating assets that can generate a return for an indefinite period. Authors, course creators, and coaches fit into this category. A course creator could spend the time (input) creating the original course and then be able to distribute it to an unlimited number of people and generate revenue. Okay, there would still need to be some time input to market the course, deal with any support issues and so on, but they have much more leverage because of the asset they created that can be sold indefinitely to an unlimited number of people.

Depending on how coaches set up their coaching programs and structures, they can position themselves in a similar way. Group coaching enables multiple people to be served and supported at the same time, and I've been a participant in many programs which have this structure. There's an opportunity to get support with your specific concerns while also listening to others and grabbing gold nuggets from them and how their concerns get responded to.

These are the reasons I made the switch from focusing on projects to identifying how to generate leverage and help more people. This book is one method — it's written and you are now reading it. Hundreds and thousands of people could all be reading it at the same time, or at any time, which means I can support people indefinitely and an unlimited number of people.

The coaching programs and courses I have created follow a similar pattern to this. For example, there is a course which sits alongside this book that has video content of the TALE Grid exercise, explanations of the 12 chains, and the other exercises in this book. It's more expensive than the book because the content delivery is different and there are a few added extras that can't be delivered via the written word.

An audiobook version of this book would further increase my leverage because the time input to create the audiobook version would not be that great compared with the ability to deliver that content to people who prefer listening than reading.

So, it's important to think about how you can use your time to create leverage because having leverage will enable you to more quickly move towards your dreams and work those 4-hour days, or have the flexibility to work whenever you want, or not have to worry about being in an office in a specific location, or be trading your time for money.

And here's a side exercise for you. Spend some time thinking about all the skills and experiences you have, and your areas of interest, and how you could turn those into a business or way of working in each of the "Routes" in the table in this chapter. It might just spark something that enables you to start breaking free of the 9-5.

# Taking Massive Action

We have the vision and goals for our future, we understand the 12 chains and how they hold us back, and we understand the 4 steps to break through the chains and move forward.

Now we need to start taking massive action and this is something that Tony Robbins talks about. When I attended his Unleash the Power Within virtual event in the summer of 2022, this was probably the biggest message I took away from the event. If we don't take massive action and start to make changes in our lives, then nothing will change. We'll continue to feel stuck, to feel frustrated, and to feel like the world is against us.

The definition of insanity is doing the same thing over and over again and expecting a different result. If we want a different experience in our lives, we need to be different and behave differently.

There are 3 things we can control in life — our thoughts, how we respond to situations, and the actions we take. It could be argued that these are actually all the same thing but, for the purpose of the exercise in this chapter, I've split them all out separately.

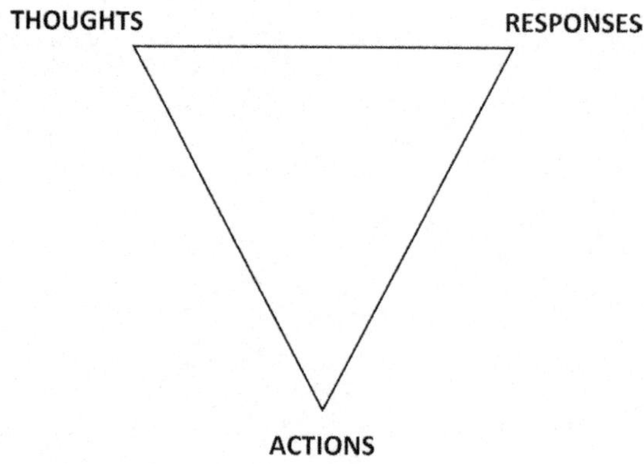

We know that habits can take 60 days to build, we know that convenience is a chain that holds us back and the types of activities that sit within this chain, we know the knowledge gap we may need to fill, and the relationships we need to focus on or move away from.

Taking massive action is now about introducing and repeating, steps 3 and 4, in the 4-step process for breaking the chains.

As Prof. Dweck, whom I referenced earlier, writes in her book — ***'Research shows that vowing, even intense vowing, is often useless. What works is making a vivid, concrete plan.'*** That plan should include consideration for when you will do something, where you will do it and how you will do it.

And to help you with this, I've created a 90-day Freedom Tracker. This tracker is different from what you may see or have experienced elsewhere because it's based on the chains and the other activities in this book. I've also chosen 90 days with consideration for the 60 days it can take to build a new habit. Ninety days is also a good number because it relates to 3 months so that it isn't so long that it becomes overwhelming.

But before I go deeper on the Freedom Tracker, I also want to talk about short-term desires, long-term desires, and the DARE model.

## Short-Term Desire vs. Long-Term Desires

The TALE Grid exercise enabled us to list out our long-term desires in the areas of how we want to spend our time, the activities we want to do regularly, the experiences we want to have, and where we want to be located.

These are long-term because we are thinking about the future we want for our lives and what our ideal life looks like.

I like to think of short-term desire as the desire we have to do an action, which fits nicely into this chapter of taking massive action. Our short-term desire to do something is based on 3 elements — ability, reward, and ease.

There's a model that I previously created for parents when I was helping them understand how children view the world differently after playing video games. Children who play video games will be provided with rewards, like a new outfit for their character, based on their actions inside the game. But the games are also designed in a way where you can't just jump straight to the last boss fight, and if you do, you would severely struggle because you don't have the right equipment, abilities or attributes for your character. This example situation is what gives us the ability and ease elements.

***Desire = Ability x Reward x Ease***

In a video game when fighting a boss, or trying to solve a puzzle, the player's desire to win is based on their ability, the reward they will get and the ease of completing the challenge or taking the action.

If they don't have the ability or the challenge/action is really difficult, the desire will be low, regardless of the reward that's being offered. If the reward is okay and the player's ability is at a good level, and the ease of the challenge is medium, then the desire will be at a medium level.

Now let us switch to a real-world example. Taking out the trash or doing the dishes. The required ability to do these tasks is low so we would have a high ability score. It's also quite easy to do these things so our ease score would be pretty high. Where our desire to do these activities takes a hit is because the reward score is likely to be low. There's no perceived physical or monetary reward for doing these tasks even if it makes our house look tidier, pleases our spouse, or stops germs and infection. And so, because of the low perceived reward score, our desire to do those tasks is lower.

Compare that to buying a lottery ticket. We have the ability so our ability score is high, it's easy — we just walk into a store or buy online, and so the ease score is high, and the potential reward is large and so our reward score is high. This combination means our desire score is much higher than for the example of taking out the trash.

But what does this mean for us when it comes to breaking the chains?

It means that as we think about taking massive action to move towards our goals and long-term desires, there will likely be things we need to do that aren't appealing and we have no desire to do, because of our ability, the ease of the activity, or perceived lack of a reward.

And these are the things we need to take massive action against because taking massive action will help improve our ability score, find ways to make the activity easier, and move us forward.

It's also possible to cheat the system a little. I've done this on more than one occasion.

Let me tell you how it works.

It's because of our power as humans to acknowledge and cope with delayed gratification. Yes, we live in a world that's all about instant gratification but we are also able to forgo that instant reward in the pursuit of something larger.

With the activities that we need to do to move forward but have no desire to do, we can stack the rewards in our favour. The long-term reward might be something on our TALE Grid but, if we have no clarity on when we will achieve that reward, it means the reward score is likely to be low. We can introduce something that will provide a short-term reward to increase the reward score and ultimately our level of desire.

A cup of tea or coffee after sending 10 emails.

A walk in the park once we've watched a video to help close the knowledge gap.

A treat at the weekend for every episode of Netflix we DIDN'T watch.

How you choose to include short-term rewards is entirely up to you. I'm just outlining how you can tweak the model to help you take the action you need to take. And yes, you could just have a cup of coffee, walk in the park or treat yourself without doing any of those things. From my experience, it feels sweeter if we also know deep down that we've worked through something we didn't want to do and made some progress, however small.

Just like crossing off something on a "to do" list gives us a little rush inside.

Now you might be reading this thinking that there are activities that you need to do that you are fearful of doing. Fear, as we've already identified, is based on the mental pictures we create in our head, so I'd like to offer an alternative way of looking at things.

People say courage is about being fearless. It isn't. Courage is about doing the hard things even when we are fearful. Once I realised this, it became easier for me to start taking action in areas where I'd previously been reluctant. I set myself the challenge of creating a short 2-minute video every day for a year and took the massive action to record the first video. I was initially fearful of what other people would think or comment and was held back by the fear and perception chains. However, I changed my view to being courageous and starting with the first step.

And that's an important point. When I say we need to take massive action, I'm not talking about jumping off a cliff or doing a 50km swim or anything drastic like that. Massive action in the context of where we want to go is really about taking the step in the direction to where we want to be, into who we want to be, and starting a new behaviour or challenge.

In the book Atomic Habits, author James Clear talks about improving by 1% each day so that we actually build in a process of compounding effort and progress. If we can improve by 1% every day in some area of our life, we can be a completely different person in a year. This is the principle I applied to myself with the 365-day video challenge. If I created a short video every day for a year and posted it online, I could be a completely different person (comfortable making videos) and in a completely different place (growing audience, building recognition for this 12 chains model, helping more people). There was no guarantee of any of this but if I didn't try and improve by 1% every day, the definite guarantee would be that I wouldn't change and wouldn't grow.

The action we don't take guarantees that nothing changes.

I'd also like to make a side point about distraction and dissatisfaction. Nir Eyal writes about distraction being the thing we turn to when we are dissatisfied with our current situation or emotional state. We turn to something, like a tub of ice cream, or an episode, to change our emotional state and make ourselves feel better. This works in the short term, but then we often feel guilty in the long run because we give in to convenience, or take actions that we know deep down don't move us towards our goals and our vision.

An alternative way of looking at this is to use our level of dissatisfaction as a fuel to drive us towards what we want. In the same way, going to the gym makes us feel good at the end of the session. We can feel good and change our emotional state if we spend some time working on things that will move us forward. It might not be the instant emotional state change we are looking for, like a tub of ice cream, but as we've talked about delayed gratification already, this would fall into the same category.

Every time I sat down to write a chapter of this book, or spent an hour writing it, I felt great afterwards because I knew I was getting closer to finishing it and having it available to help people. This is partial gratification because I knew I was making progress and the delayed gratification is about having the book finished and available to support people.

If we can move to a space where we are comfortable with lots of delayed gratification and use our dissatisfaction as fuel, we can continue to take the action we need that will move us closer to achieving our goals and dreams.

## Preparation vs. Action

Although this chapter is about taking action, I think it's also important to understand the concept of preparation vs. action.

Preparation is the time we spend learning something, practising a skill, honing our ability, and doing all the groundwork.

We can think we are taking action, but sometimes we are in a cycle of doing preparation work. When the gun sounds at the start of a race, the lights go out at the start of an F1 race or the countdown timer says "start" in a video game, everything that happens after these points is action, everything before is about preparation.

This was highlighted to me when I went to a workshop with a series of guest speakers talking about extreme endurance. Sam Morris was one of the speakers and he talked about his rowing race across the Atlantic Ocean with two teammates.

They spent 2 years preparing for a 38-day race.

There were courses about sailing, safety, how to use the radio effectively, what to do in case of a fire, nutrition, and a long list of other things they had to learn and get certified on. They also had to spend time in the boat getting used to it, getting used to spending the night on the water and multiple days away from shore. Sam shared a long list of the things they had to learn, the prep that went into the race, and all the equipment they needed to have on the boat including food and water.

Taking courses about how to build a business, or joining my Freedom Hunters Club, and watching the video course version of this book, are examples of preparation. The move to action would be when you actually take the first step to build a business — like deciding on who your customer is, the service you are going to offer, and the name of your project. After watching the video version of this book, the action would be when you complete the activities, like the ones in this book, and start making changes in your life.

Here's what Jack Canfield says about taking action:

> ***"When you take action, you trigger all kinds of things that will inevitably carry you to success. You let those around you know that you are serious in your intention. People wake up and start paying attention."***

Thinking will only get us so far. If we truly want to live a life of freedom and achieve the things we've written in our TALE Grid, we will need to take action.

## Considerations, Fear, and Roadblocks

I also want to pay respect to Jack Canfield for the line of thinking I'm about to take you through in this mini-topic. In his book, he outlined considerations, fears, and roadblocks as things that get presented to us when we start to take action.

Considerations are the thoughts we think that may make us pause for a moment and reassess a situation or our approach.

Fears are things that may genuinely stop us from taking action, like a phobia, rather than the mental images we create as I outlined in the chapter about the chain of fear.

And then roadblocks are the things that get in our way, slow us down, and may prevent us from making progress. But roadblocks are also things that can be overcome, or worked around, by finding a different route or option.

This is the bit that I wanted to highlight in this mini-topic. Roadblocks are not a stone wall, they are a fence with a sign that says "Sorry, not this way" which redirects you to other opportunities and ways of working or operating.

I'm going to use a business example in an attempt to make this a little clearer.

Say you want to get in contact with the CEO of a company because you want to do business with them. You have a product and service that's so extraordinary you could save this CEO thousands of dollars, and his staff a lot of time.

You try phoning the front desk to get his contact number and email address, but you are brushed off with a comment of company policy not permitting those details to be shared.

Now you've hit a roadblock. Your first attempt to make contact with the CEO didn't work so you've got to find a different way. You could send a hand-written letter to him in the post, you could send a message on LinkedIn, or you could try to find out if you have any mutual connections who could do a warm introduction. These are all ways of working around the roadblock.

Roadblocks are not permanent and shouldn't stop you in your tracks; they are just a redirect. This sort of thinking is echoed by Matthew McConaughey in his book 'Green Lights' where he talks about red, yellow, and green lights. A roadblock could be a yellow light that's actually helping steer you in a different and better direction for what you want to achieve. The "Sorry, not this way" sign might lead you to a single conversation that completely changes your life.

And if we maintain a positive and growth mindset, it becomes easier to identify the roadblocks for exactly what they are, rather than falling into a pit of despair because we think the sign in front of us is telling us to cancel our dreams.

We can and should embrace the roadblocks because they are part of the journey and can lead us to bigger and better things.

## Your Freedom Tracker

Now that we understand the DARE model and how we can play with our levels of desire for doing the tasks and activities that we need to do to move forward, we've reframed taking massive action, and we understand the difference between preparation and action, let's go back to the Freedom Tracker.

What exactly is this Freedom Tracker and how does it use the activities we've completed in previous chapters?

I'm glad you asked.

Each tracker sheet charts 31 days in little boxes so you have the ability to cross off each day for a month. This also means you would have one sheet per month so that after a 90-day period, you can compare what has happened each month and your progress. The thing that makes this tracker different is because of what you write in each row that you want to do more of or do less of. And there are sections focused on several of the chains we've talked about in this book.

In the top section for "do more of" there are two rows labelled ACT, two labelled REL, and two labelled KN. The rows for ACT are about the activities that you want to do more of. You would write in the box a short description of the activity — like "walk for 30 minutes", "walk 10,000 steps", "record a short video" or something similar depending on the activities you want to focus on, that will make you feel good, or move you closer to your goals.

The other rows follow a similar pattern — in the rows labelled REL, you will write the people who fuel you and you want to spend more time with. The KN rows are for the knowledge you want to gain to help you make progress towards your goals and vision for the future.

There are also 2 empty rows giving you the space to write in extra activities, relationships, or knowledge that you want to focus on for the month block, or anything else that's important for you to track.

Then in the bottom section, it's about the things you want to do less of, or the people you want to see less of because they drain you. There are 3 rows labelled CV which are about the conveniences that you want to cut down on with the 3 rows for REL being the relationships and people you want to see less of. Like the top section, you also have extra rows to write down other conveniences, relationships, or responsibilities that you want to do less of.

I purposefully didn't create rows for responsibilities and priorities because we've identified those as being external influences and they might require some negotiation. Knowledge, Conveniences, Activities, and Relationships are things we have more control over such as how we use our time, our focus, and our energy.

Finally, there's a box at the bottom for writing notes about some of the experiences you had during the month for the rows in the tracker. You could write about the things that went well, or not so well, the situations that meant you saw someone you didn't want to, or how you are building a routine where you do something at the same time every day to build consistency.

And now that we have the outline of the different parts of the Freedom Tracker, I want to provide clarity on how to use and complete this tracker.

In the main section of "do more of" you will check the boxes for each day you DO that action.

Then in the section of "do less of" you will check the boxes for the days you DON'T do that thing.

Here are two images showing you what I mean with an example. The tracker is available in the resource pack that I've mentioned throughout this book — you can download it here www.finallyfindfreedom.com/resources.

| DO MORE OF | | Day 1 | 2 | 3 | 4 | 5 | 6 | 7 | 8 | 9 | Day 10 | 11 | 12 | 13 | 14 | 15 |
|---|---|---|---|---|---|---|---|---|---|---|---|---|---|---|---|---|
| ACT | 2-min vid each day | x | x | x | x | x | x | x | x | x | x | x | x | x | x | x |
| ACT | Message 20 people | x | x | x | | | | x | x | x | | | | x | x | x |
| REL | Mum & Dad | x | | | | | | x | | | | | | | x | |
| REL | Andy | | x | | | | | | x | | | | | | | x |
| KN | 1 chpt a day (biz) | x | x | x | x | x | x | x | x | x | x | x | x | x | x | x |
| KN | Immigration | x | | | | | | | x | x | | | | | | |
| | | | | | | | | | | | | | | | | |
| | | | | | | | | | | | | | | | | |

What we can see in the first image is part of the "do more of" section. I've written in items for breaking the knowledge chain, fuelling relationships, and the routines/habits I want to create.

In the rows for activities (ACT), I've written that I want to create a daily 2-minute video and message 20 people. For relationships (REL), I've put my mum and dad, and a good friend called Andy.

I've already referenced in this book that I set myself a year-long challenge to record and post a 2-minute video each day to prove to myself that I can be consistent. So, in this row, I've checked/marked each day that I recorded a video and posted.

For the activities row of sending messages to 20 people, I've checked some of the boxes. I wasn't able to do this every day based on other things happening in my life but that's okay. At the end of the month, I can see how much I have done and I'll also be able to determine what impact that has had — like new and interesting conversations or insights from the people I sent those messages to.

In the relationship (REL) rows, I don't have as many boxes checked because I wasn't able to see those people all the time, but you will notice I've been able to get into a sort of pattern with a checked box every week. This is an example of building a routine with the person who fuels you so that you can regularly have contact with them and continue to build that relationship.

Then in the rows for knowledge (KN), I've written that I want to read 1 chapter each day of a business book and I want to learn more about immigration. This will be the immigration laws and considerations for the desert island or country I want to be based in that I originally wrote into my TALE Grid.

The daily chapter I was able to do so, I've checked those boxes, and the boxes for breaking the knowledge chain about immigration, which I was able to do on a few different days. Only checking a few boxes for a knowledge row is okay because it's not something that I needed to do every day — there's only so much information I might need about this topic and once I have it, I can move onto another area of knowledge I want to gain.

This top section of the Freedom Tracker is the easiest to use because it's a case of if you do it, you tick the box.

The bottom section for "do less of" is a little bit of a reversal and will take a bit of getting used to. You mark the days you don't do whatever activity you don't do, the person you don't see, or things you said you wanted to do less of. This gives you the opportunity to add more ticks or crosses and demonstrate progress.

Progress in the context of "do less of" is exactly that — you make progress by doing less of the things you said you wanted to do less of. This means the more ticks or crosses you have in this section, the more progress you are making and living up to what you said you wanted to do.

| DO LESS OF | | Day 1 | 2 | 3 | 4 | 5 | 6 | 7 | 8 | 9 | Day 10 | 11 | 12 | 13 | 14 | 15 |
|---|---|---|---|---|---|---|---|---|---|---|---|---|---|---|---|---|
| CV | Netflix (< 2 hr) | x | x | x | x | x | | x | x | x | x | | x | x | x | x |
| CV | No takeaway | x | x | x | x | x | x | x | x | x | x | x | x | x | x | x |
| CV | | | | | | | | | | | | | | | | |
| REL | Sarah | x | x | x | x | x | x | x | | x | x | x | x | x | x | |
| REL | Mark | x | x | x | x | x | x | | x | x | x | x | x | x | x | x |
| REL | John at work | x | x | x | x | x | x | x | x | x | x | | x | x | x | x |
| | | | | | | | | | | | | | | | | |
| | | | | | | | | | | | | | | | | |

This second image is from the "do less of" section. There's a row for the people I want to spend less time with and the convenience items I want to spend less time doing. Where I've checked the boxes it's because I didn't do those things.

In the convenience (CV) rows, I've written that I want to spend 2 hours or less watching Netflix and not have a takeaway. In the relationship (REL) rows, I put some random names down for people.

If we look at the convenience rows, you will see I was able to say "no" to having a takeaway every day — I DIDN'T do that thing and so I've checked the box. For Netflix, there are a couple of days I haven't checked because I didn't meet my goal — I spent more than 2 hours watching because a film was longer than 2 hours so I need to leave the box blank.

And underneath, I've made some notes in the Notes box about the things that happened — like seeing Sarah at a group meeting and that maybe I need to find a different group to join so I don't see her or spend time with her, that the Netflix films put me over my 2-hour goal, and that I only saw John when he came into the office and that's something I can cope with.

| NOTES | Sarah was at the group meeting every week, might need to change groups<br>John came into the office, but only as part of the project<br>Was able to avoid having a takeaway<br>Few days where I slipped with Netflix and watched a film that went over the 2-hour limit. |
|---|---|

The whole point of this Freedom Tracker is so that we have a visual record of the progress we are making in key areas — the knowledge we want to gain, activities we want to do, and the relationships we want to strengthen, along with the things we want to do less of.

It also enables us to start seeing patterns and situations that we may want to take further action against. I already mentioned that if I did this tracker for the next month, my knowledge row may change from immigration to something else, like buying a property, because I had all the knowledge I needed about immigration. So, the next thing on my list to support my TALE Grid was understanding purchasing property in the country I had chosen.

Which is why I also suggest doing the Freedom Tracker in 90-day "seasons". If you keep recording things in 90-day seasons, you'll be able to look back over time and see which items you've successfully done more of, and which you've successfully done less of, and any patterns where you might have slipped a little, or if there were situations that meant it became more challenging to "do more" or "do less".

I also want to briefly talk about the judgment calls you may need to make about what constitutes a "do less" action. Here's an example — if it's

Netflix, it can be tough if the action is a shared experience with a spouse or family so perhaps it's not about cutting out entirely, perhaps it's just 1 episode instead of 3. For this, you'd write something like "1 episode or less" in a convenience (CV) row in the "do less of" section of the tracker and that's what you would look to check the boxes based on.

Ultimately, it is about how honest you are with yourself, the vision, goals and dreams you have for your life, and how willing you are to be consistent and persistent in the face of any adversity.

—

## ACTIVITY #9 – Start Your Freedom Tracker

*Using the template for the Freedom Tracker, write into the top section the Activities (ACT), Relationships (REL), and Knowledge (KN) that you want to focus on for the next month.*

*Now, under the bottom section of "do less of" write in the rows of Convenience (CV) and Relationships (REL) the things and people you want to do less of, and see less of.*

*Next, put your ticks or crosses in the appropriate boxes*

*1) Check each box when you DO a "do more of" item and row*

*2) Check a box when you DON'T do a "do less of" item and row.*

*Do this each day of the month and write down any notes that you feel are relevant such as the patterns you've noticed or the situations where you were able to do more or do less.*

*Continue the Freedom Tracker for 3 months and review your progress to see what new habits and behaviours you've started to build and what's taking you closer to your dreams and goals, and how consistent you've been.*

*Also, review how you've been progressing in the "do less of" area, what impact that's had on your life, and what you can do better for the next season.*

—

I also want to give a word about integration. From reading this book, you will have gained the focus and clarity on what you want to achieve, how you want to live, and how you want to spend your time, but that doesn't always mean everyone is on the same page as you.

Making radical changes can upset the apple cart and cause some friction, so it's important to let other people know that you are working to make some changes and that may mean some changes in actions, behaviour, and how you want to spend your time. This will probably be alien to the people around you to begin with, as was the situation when I gave up alcohol, but over time those people will become more comfortable with it, and they may even appreciate the changes you start to make.

If you want to dive a little deeper into this topic of integration, there is a great podcast episode between Ajit Nawalka and Kole Whitty which talks through her journey of integration after being in a coma from drugs, physical challenges, and other experiences in her life. You can find it by searching for the "Master Coaching with Ajit" podcast and its episode number 146.

I'd also love to hear how you get on with the Freedom Tracker, or if you have suggestions for changes after you've been using it for a while. The objective is to provide you with the starting point and then empower you to evolve it as you make changes in your life and make progress towards freedom.

And so, now we head to the final chapter of this book where we look at two extra tools you can use on your journey.

# Finally Finding FREEDOM

Freedom is subjective for all of us.

What freedom means to me and how I want to live my life is likely to be very different from you. There may be some common threads or trends and the research I did as I started to write this book had spending time with family as a key focus for a lot of the respondents.

So if freedom is different for everyone, how can we achieve it?

It isn't like us all taking the same exam or test and knowing there is always a set of correct answers or knowledge we need to ace the test.

Instead, I like to think about it as a set of guiding principles and I guess the 12 chains fit into that category. Throughout this book, we've explored each of the 12 chains that hold us back. We've then looked at the 3 different types of chains, which type is the easiest to break first, and the 4 steps that help us break any chain.

Putting this all together into a simplified format is something I've done for myself to help me remember and to keep me focused.

After another one of my coffee sessions with my headphones on, I looked at the letters of the word freedom and started thinking about what each of them could mean to create a memorable phrase or set of words.

I also thought about what freedom means to me and how I see myself achieving freedom in my own life. And that's when I turned the word freedom into a phrase and acrostic.

Here it is.

F = Focused
R = Repetition
E = Enables
E = Experiences
D = Desires
O = Opportunities and
M = Money

Or for the full phrase — "Focused repetition enables experiences, desires, opportunities, and money."

Changing our behaviours and removing some of the conveniences means we can replace them with new activities or experiences. Using that time to gain knowledge and break the knowledge chain can open up new opportunities. And creating a new habit can take time which is why we need focused repetition.

Focused repetition is also important for generating money to be able to have the experiences and fulfil desires. This focused repetition might be writing a book, learning and using a skill to build a business, like how I talked about what Dino and Eddy had done with Twitter/X, or it might be showing up every day to serve and support coaching clients. There are many ways to position and think about focused repetition but, at the core, it is about creating those new habits and doing the things that will move us forward towards the vision we've created for ourselves.

I also want to quickly provide you with a mantra or saying you can use with your meditation if that's something that appeals to you. You could also print it out and stick it on a wall or on your desk next to your TALE Grid.

Here it is:

*"I recognise that there may be gaps in my* ***KNOWLEDGE*** *that currently hold me back from achieving what I want but that I can fill those gaps. I understand that the* ***SPEED*** *at which I operate will influence how quickly I can live the life I desire. I accept that* ***CONVENIENCE*** *is everywhere and that I have the power to choose my actions. I can identify and manage* ***RELATIONSHIPS*** *that both drain and energise me so that I always feel fuelled.*

*I recognise that other people may want to give me* ***RESPONSIBILITY*** *and that their* ***PRIORITIES*** *may not be my own but that I can take control of how I use my* ***TIME*** *and where I am* ***LOCATED****.*

*I understand that actions have* ***RISK*** *but that* ***FEAR*** *is an image in my mind that I can change. I will not give in to* ***PRESSURE*** *from others and I will not be influenced by other people's* ***PERCEPTION*** *of me because I know the TALE that I want to tell of my life and I welcome the journey to get there.*

*Through focused repetition of identifying and breaking the chains that are holding me back, I will enable the experiences, desires, opportunities, and money to come to me now and in the future."*

This is something I started using myself after I wrote it for the first time because it helped me get clarity.

For me, it reinforced that I have the power in my life and the ability to make changes. You too have that same power.

I also want to highlight the section "because I know the TALE that I want to tell of my life, and I welcome the journey to get there."

This is important because we need to recognise that life is a journey. The experiences on the way make us who we are. If I hadn't broken my neck and decided to start making changes, or found the advert on YouTube for a personal development course, or made the decision to move to the UAE, then this book would not exist.

It is all a journey and once we accept that, it becomes easier to let go of the things that don't serve us and to embrace the uncomfortable steps we need to take to move to the next step on that journey. In one online webinar, I listened to the host make reference to taking a leap of faith and that sometimes it's like jumping from a cliff without being able to see a bridge or way to get to the other side. Those who take the leap of faith trust that the bridge will appear, or be built, as they need it.

Once we can see past the constructs of society that are not serving us, and we can look down and see the chains that bind us, that's when we can start making those changes.

They say ignorance is bliss. That you don't know what you don't know. Both of which can be true from a certain point of view. And that's why my objective has been to help you see the chains clearly because once you see them, you cannot unsee them. They will always be in the back of your mind and enable you to question things. Question if something is serving you, question whether taking an action will move you forward, question whether the relationship is a positive one or not, and question whether you are being pressured or giving into the perceptions of others.

These are all things you now have the power and the tools to break free from.

I'm excited to see where you go and what you can do.

And I'd like to congratulate you on making it this far and welcome you into a special club.

By reading this book, completing the activities, and starting to make changes in your life, you have officially become a FREEDOM HUNTER.

A FREEDOM HUNTER is defined as someone who is:

***An unusually committed visionary***

***Who's tired of the rat race, feeling stuck in their life, and frustrated with all the gurus and courses that talk strategy but never the daily tactics to succeed***

***A champion who knows they are meant for more and who is willing to do whatever it takes to find their personal freedom***

***Prioritises their time and energy over the constraints and BS rules of society to move from being bound in chains to being free***

Your commitment to yourself, to making changes and to living the life you want is what sets you apart.

I'd love to hear about your journey as you take the next steps and as you break free.

Speak soon.

Philip.

# One Request and One Offer for You

Firstly, thank you for taking the time to grab a copy of this book and read through it. I hope you've found it informative and it's given you clarity on areas of your life and you feel empowered to move forward.

I'd really appreciate it if you could leave a review of the book on Amazon. In order for me to help more people I need to ensure the book is visible in the Amazon algorithm. If you are reading on Kindle this could be as simple as scrolling to the end of the book and clicking the star rating you feel is most appropriate but if you are willing to take the time to write a physical review you can do that on this link (it will take you to Amazon) — https://www.finallyfindfreedom.com/review, or by using the QR code displayed here.

That's the request.

Now to the offer.

While you've been reading through this book, I've made reference to the fact that first and foremost I'm a coach focused on helping people break free of the chains, become unstuck and work towards their goals and desires.

And if you are committed to moving forward in your life, using the tools in this book, and breaking the chains but are unsure of taking the next step, or prefer to have some support, I'd like to offer you a path for consideration.

I invite you to book a call with me or a member of the team for free, with no obligation, so that you can get a different perspective on the chains you feel are holding you back and the suggested best next steps.

There are a limited number of calls available, and they are available on a first-come, first-serve basis.

It's also great if you've created your TALE Grid, which is the first exercise in this book, as it gives us a starting point for the discussion.

You can book your call here — https://www.finallyfindfreedom.com/call

# Connect With Me on Social Media

If you are interested in connecting with me on social media, I have accounts on the majority of platforms. I've also provided links below to the podcast and the YouTube channel so you can easily find them.

New podcast episodes are released every week and the YouTube channel includes videos of the podcast interviews, daily thoughts, training on topics related to the 12 chains and finding freedom, and recordings of live workshops or speaking sessions.

—

You can also find all these links on this URL — https://www.finallyfindfreedom.com/social or by scanning the QR code below.

# Books on My Reading List

These are books I've read and found useful for learning, or drawn inspiration from, and that you might find of equal value now that you've finished this book. These are books I re-read on a semi-regular basis and find I view them in a new light as I grow and change, and the world around me changes.

- 'Mindset — Changing the Way You Think to Fulfil Your Potential' by Professor Caroline Dweck
- 'The Code of The Extraordinary Mind' by Vishen Lakhiani
- 'Atomic Habits' by James Clear
- 'Indistractable' by Nir Eyal
- 'How To Get to From Where You Are to Where You Want to Be' by Jack Canfield
- 'The Greatest Salesman in The World' by OG Mandino
- 'The Power of Now' by Eckart Tolle
- 'Negotiating Like Your Life Depended on It' by Chris Voss
- 'Think And Grow Rich' by Napoleon Hill
- '$100M Offers: How to Make Offers So Good People Feel Stupid Saying No' by Alex Hormozi
- 'Expert Secrets' by Russell Brunson
- 'The Chimp Paradox' by Professor Steve Peters

# Appendix – Meditation Practices, Morning Routines and Time Management Tools

We've covered the main thoughts for this book already with the 12 chains and the steps you can take to break them, but here in the Appendix, I wanted to give you some additional tools and practices you can use on your journey.

But this first appendix is about tools and practices for meditation, morning routines, and time management tools.

In the main chunk of the book, I mentioned the 6-phase meditation from Vishen Lakhiani and below is a summary of the 6 phases you go through during this meditation. In total, it is 20 minutes long and a great way to set yourself up for the day.

Here's a summary of the 6 phases of this meditation. You can also find videos about it on YouTube by searching for "6 phase meditation".

–

**Love and Compassion:** In this phase, you are guided through an exercise to have compassion for all living things on earth. You start by thinking about where you live, then your neighbourhood, city, and country while sending your love and compassion out to those places.

**Happiness and Gratitude:** Gratitude is about acknowledging and appreciating the abundance in your life. In this phase, you think about the positive things that have happened in your personal life or your work life over the previous period — a day, a week, a year.

**Peace and Forgiveness:** Forgiveness involves releasing any negative emotions or grudges you may be holding, towards yourself or others. You picture someone who has wronged you and you read out a list of charges against them. Then you switch roles and see things from their perspective and why they might have wronged you.

**Vision For Your Future:** Here, you tap into the power of visualization to manifest your dreams and goals. You think about your goals 3 years from now and what it is you want to achieve. You imagine them being played out like a movie on a screen in front of you.

**Mastering Your Day:** In this phase, you set your intentions for the day by thinking about segments. You picture your morning segment and how you want it to unfold and then add in your other senses such as sound and smell. You repeat this for all the segments of your day.

**Daily Blessing:** In this final phase, you ask for your daily blessing and call down a beam of light through your body and into the earth. The blessing has the power and everything you need for your day ahead.

—

I try to do this a few times a week because it has the phases of compassion, gratitude, and forgiveness which are not things that I tend to do in other meditation practices — most of the others are about visions for the future and the perfect day.

Other ones that I've done and found useful include Marissa Peer's "Guided Hypnosis for creating a new empowering belief system". This helps to re-wire your brain and mindset by getting you to repeat positive comments to yourself and leverage the neuroplasticity that we talked about previously. Marissa is known as one of the world's best hypnotherapists and counts royalty, pop stars, and A-list celebs as her clients.

There are thousands of meditation routines and recordings available on the internet so it is worth spending some time to find one that suits you. I'm personally not someone who is into spirituality, even if I believe the universe has a plan, so those sorts of meditations don't work for me. I can't connect with them.

In terms of morning routines, for me personally, this varies depending on what I've got going on. Sometimes it's the walk to the golf club and being out in nature while listening to a podcast, other times it is just the meditation and then I get stuck into whatever it is that I'm focusing on for the day. But one thing that's helped me, and also plays into the time management discussion, is about having consistency around key elements.

The walk and meditation set me up nicely for the day ahead because they are both calming and help me feel centred. There's no rush involved in them. I can do them and take the time I need. I also try to stop myself from looking at my emails, or responding, until 9 am so that the time before 9 am is dedicated to me.

When I spoke to Caren Paskel for the Unchained podcast, she told me she'd created a 4-hour morning routine that included being in nature and yoga and a few other things. She didn't start "work" until 11 am so that she had time for herself.

Think about what's important to you and what will help you set yourself up for success each day — maybe it is a meditation practice in the morning, maybe it's just saying mantras and affirmations to put yourself into a positive state of mind, maybe it is taking some time in nature.

Which leads me to time management. I mentioned time boxing and habit stacking, so now I want to provide a little more detail on each of those so you have a complete picture. I know I'm at my most creative first thing in the morning so this is when I do my focus work, or the work that needs deep thinking. The majority of this book was written in 2-hour chunks in the morning at coffee shops around Dubai. Making notes about projects and responding to project briefs, or writing the slides for proposals, has always been done in the morning when my creative juices are flowing best. I time box this in so that in my calendar, I have time allocated for this type of work. When I book calls, I try to schedule them for after 11 am so that I have this focus time available first thing.

Habit stacking becomes easier when you are intentional with your time, or you use something like time boxing, and know when certain things are going to happen in your day.

If you create a morning routine with a few key things in it, you have the knowledge of the order you do those things and how long they take. With this, you could introduce new things straight after each activity in your routine, or at the end of your routine.

I encourage you to try time boxing and habit stacking, especially if there are things you've written on your Freedom Tracker that you want to do more or do less of. Time boxing them in can help you find the time for them (do more), or restrict the time for them (do less) if you've set a time allocation.

The final note on this part of this appendix is that my practices and preferences have changed over time so the bits that I've written in this appendix are the "here and now" as I've written this book. They may change in the future and that may be true for you as well — you may try something and then find something different that works better. That's perfectly okay and I encourage you to embrace that process because it means you are changing and growing.

# Appendix – Book Activities

As you read through the book, there were some suggested activities to help you gain clarity on the current state of things in your life which was Step 1 (Assess) in the 4-step framework for breaking the chains.

I've provided the activity descriptions here again for reference so that you can come back to them at any time without needing to continually flick through the book trying to find them.

This will enable you to keep track and also identify any activities that you might have missed while you were reading.

And as I've mentioned throughout the book, there's a free resource pack with templates you can use for each of these activities and it's available at www.finallyfindfreedom.com/resources or you can scan the QR code below.

## ACTIVITY #1 – Create Your TALE Grid

*I've given you some pointers already but now it is time to write in your TALE Grid. If you've downloaded the supporting resources, you have a template to use.*

*If not, then creating the grid on a piece of A4 paper is quick and easy. Just draw a line down the middle of the page, and then across the middle of the page. This will give you your 4 quadrants and then in each one, write one of the words: TIME, ACTIVITIES, LOCATION, EXPERIENCES.*

*The next step is to write down the relevant things to you in each of the quadrants by following the instructions in this chapter. How do you want to spend your time and how much time do you want to spend working? How much time with family each day? Where in the world do you want to be located? What activities do you want to do regularly? And what experiences do you want to have in your life?*

*If you are a business owner, entrepreneur, or wanting to break free of the 9-5, think about where you'd love your business to be located, whether you want team and staff activities in your grid like day trips away, and how you split your time between your business and your home life.*

*This is personal to you and the TALE Grid is something we will refer back to throughout this book so I encourage you to take a little time to create it.*

—

## ACTIVITY #2 – Assess the Knowledge Gap

*I've just talked about breaking the knowledge chain by filling the gap in the knowledge I needed for publishing a book on Amazon. Now it's your turn.*

*Based on your TALE Grid, create a list of all the knowledge you think you'll need to support you in achieving the items in your grid.*

*If you've written down that you want to live somewhere different, think about those fun things like taxation and immigration. Think about the cost of living and visas.*

*The goal is not to overwhelm you which I appreciate could be the case if you have a long list, but overwhelm only happens if you let it. Instead, see your list as a "to do" list and things that you can work towards and cross off. You don't need to have everything crossed off by tomorrow, but at least you now have a guiding list of the knowledge that will support you in achieving the things in your TALE Grid.*

*We will also be coming back to this list in a later chapter of the book.*

—

## ACTIVITY #3 – 7-Day Activity Log

*This activity is about helping you identify where you currently fall into the trap of convenience. I know it can be scary to create something that slaps you in the face and tells you that you might be wasting time, but the first step for making a change is to assess where we are currently.*

*If we can identify the activities we spend time on and have it in black and white, it becomes easier to start making a change.*

*For a 7-day period, write down every activity you do during the day and how much time you spend on it. This should include mealtimes, work, sleeping, walking the dog, watching Netflix, playing with the kids, basically anything you do.*

*If you are a business owner, or entrepreneur, write down the different types of meetings you have and how much time you spend on them. These could be daily stand-up meetings, sales meetings, appraisals, or any other type of meeting.*

*One of the things I wish I'd done a long time ago was start to log the time I spent writing proposals and presentations that went nowhere. I could have spent that time focusing on something else to grow my business in a different way.*

*If you've downloaded the extra resource pack, you will have seen a sheet to act as your activity log. If not, then you can use an A4 piece of paper and draw 7 columns with a label for each day of the week. Then write in each column the activities you do each day and, in a bracket or circle, next to them, how much time you spent doing them.*

*Like the list of knowledge we've identified, we need to gain this activity log. It's something we'll come back to in a later chapter when we start looking at how to break the chains.*

—

## ACTIVITY #4 – Assessing Our Relationships

*For this activity, there's also a premade sheet in the downloadable resource pack, but if you haven't got it, then take another A4 piece of paper and write down all the names of the people you spend 2 or more hours with each month.*

*This includes people you work with. If you are a business owner or entrepreneur, this can include employees, business partners, and clients.*

*Once you have your list, I want you to score each person on a scale of 1 to 10. A score of 1 is really negative and draining while a score of 10 is a relationship and person that fuels you and brings you joy.*

*Now we can see if there are any patterns — like groups of people at work or in the office, family members or friends who either drain or fuel us.*

*Like the previous activities, this is a list we will keep for later so don't lose it.*

—

## ACTIVITY #5 – Assessing Our Priorities

*This chapter has looked at the two different types of priorities and so this activity is about writing them down.*

*The downloadable resource has a sheet split into 2 with a column for you to write your own priorities and the things you deem are important. The second column is for those activities and "priorities" given to you by other people that aren't actually your priorities.*

*This can be a little tricky because we often accept other people's priorities as our own, but if we look deep down and ask the question "which would I rather do?" you will be able to identify your own priorities and those given to you by other people. You can also do it by asking the question of where did the priority originate from — you or someone else.*

—

## ACTIVITY #6 – Assessing Your Responsibilities

*Much like Activity #5, this activity is about creating the comparison between those responsibilities you wanted, requested, and willingly took on versus those responsibilities that were handed to you.*

*Using the downloadable sheet, write in each of the columns which responsibilities you have that you wanted and are still happy to do, and which were given to you or you no longer want to do.*

*If you don't have the downloadable resource pack, then writing two columns on a piece of paper will work just as well. You can label the columns "Positive" and "Negative" to denote the two different types of responsibilities we are talking about.*

*Keep these lists safe with all your scribbles from the other activities as we will be coming back to them.*

—

## ACTIVITY #7 – Assessing Our Fears

*For this activity, I'd like you to write a list of all the things you fear about moving towards the items on your TALE Grid. This could be moving country and the mental image you create of it all going wrong. Or the mental image you create about changing jobs. Or the mental image of starting your own business and not getting any clients.*

*It doesn't matter what the fears are, or the mental images you've created as your worst case, this activity is about writing them down and recognising the "what ifs" that are flowing around in your head.*

*Once we have them on paper, we can start to address them when we look at the 4 steps to breaking the chains.*

—

## ACTIVITY #8 – Create a Do More/Do Less List

*On a piece of paper, create two columns and at the top of one, write "Do More Of" and at the top of the other, write "Do Less Of".*

*Now, under each heading, write a list of the activities that you want to do more and do less of.*

*These lists can be anything you like, some taken from your TALE Grid, others may come from your 7-day Activity Log.*

—

## ACTIVITY #9 – Start Your Freedom Tracker

*Using the template for the Freedom Tracker, write into the top section the Activities (ACT), Relationships (REL), and Knowledge (KN) that you want to focus on for the next month.*

*Now, under the bottom section of "do less of", write in the rows of Convenience (CV) and Relationships (REL) the things and people you want to do less of, and see less of.*

*Next, put your ticks or crosses in the appropriate boxes*

*1) Check each box when you DO a "do more of" item and row*

*2) Check a box when you DON'T do a "do less of" item and row*

*Do this each day of the month and write down any notes that you feel are relevant such as the patterns you've noticed or the situations where you were able to do more or do less.*

*Continue the Freedom Tracker for 3 months and review your progress to see what new habits and behaviours you've started to build and what's taking you closer to your dreams and goals, and how consistent you've been.*

*Also, review how you've been progressing in the "do less of" area, what impact that's had on your life, and what you can do better for the next season.*

—

# Acknowledgements

Writing a book isn't just about the author getting the words onto the page. Support comes in many different forms so I'd like to take a moment to acknowledge some of the people who have supported the journey of getting this book written and published.

Firstly, a big thank you to Hannah and my Mum and Dad for their continued support, even when they thought I was crazy for wanting to move away from the video game industry.

To Nick who provided guidance on the best way to set the book up for success.

My podcast guests and coaches who gave me their stories and helped shape some of the chapters including Freddie, Caren, Johanna, Neil, Paul, Shane, Don, Chloe, Zai, and Alison.

All those who helped with my research and completed the survey asking about their visions for life.

To my launch team who helped with the early momentum and to all the members of the Freedom Hunters Club.

And to you, for taking the time to read this far and for letting me be a small part of your journey and your personal story.

Printed in Great Britain
by Amazon